BOOK OF
CAKES & DESSERTS

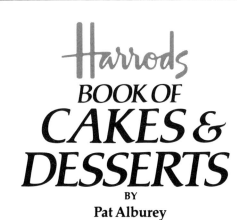

Harrods
BOOK OF
CAKES &
DESSERTS

BY

Pat Alburey

**ARBOR
HOUSE**

NEW YORK

Published by Ebury Press
Division of The National Magazine Company Ltd
Colquhoun House
27–37 Broadwick Street
London W1V 1FR

First Impression 1986

Published in the United States of America by
Arbor House Publishing Company
and in Canada by Fitzhenry & Whiteside Ltd
by arrangement with Ebury Press, London

———◆———

EDITORS: Fiona MacIntyre, Felicity Jackson, Susan Friedland
ART DIRECTOR: Frank Phillips
DESIGNER: Marshall Art
PHOTOGRAPHY: Grant Symon
STYLIST: Sue Russell
HOME ECONOMISTS: Susanna Tee, Janet Smith and Maxine Clark

Ebury Press would like to thank Harrods, and their archivist
Margaret Baber, for allowing the use of the black and white
illustrations taken from Harrods catalogues.

Library of Congress Cataloging-in-Publication Data

Alburey, Pat.
    Harrods book of cake and desserts.

    1. Cake. 2. Desserts. I. Harrods Ltd. II. Title.
TX771.A49   1986   641.8'653   86-8020
ISBN 0-87795-819-X

Computerset by MFK Typesetting Ltd, Hitchin, Herts
Printed and bound in Italy by New Interlitho Spa, Milan

Contents

*All eggs used in this book are
large unless otherwise stated.*

Introduction

HOWEVER splendid the previous courses may have been, it is, without doubt, the dessert that creates the most impression and is the course most eagerly awaited. Its choice must be considered with great deliberation, so as not to disappoint those who eagerly await its arrival. But it must be chosen to complement the rest of the meal, not to take all the applause.

Cooking is all about tempting and pleasing the appetite, and the most important factor to remember when choosing a dessert is that it is served at the end of the meal, when appetites are waning. With a few exceptions, a dessert does not have an aroma to help stimulate the appetite, it relies purely on the visual senses.

Presentation is everything – desserts must look as exquisite as possible, so that in delighting the eye, the appetite will be tempted. But it must not be too elaborate, or the thought of eating it may be overwhelming. A softly frozen sherbet, elegantly served, can have as much impact, and be even more welcome, than an elaborate pastry creation lavishly decorated with cream. It all depends on what has gone before.

The dessert should complement the main courses in both flavor and color, and provide a contrast in texture. Don't serve a meat pie followed by a pastry dessert. Main courses consisting of soft textures should be followed by a dessert with a crisp or crunchy texture. Crêpes after pasta would be wrong, a fresh salad, or light meringue cake would be better.

The dessert should not contain any distinctive ingredient used in the previous courses. When main courses contain a lot of cream, avoid using it for the dessert. Follow creamy foods with a more sharply flavored dessert and spicy foods with creamy ones.

Always consider the occasion and be wary of mingling elaborate dishes with homey ones. A plain omelet and salad would be best followed by something like an apple pie, but that same pie served as the climax to a celebration dinner for 12 would look very out of place; a beautifully molded bavarois would be more fitting for a formal occasion.

Colors should complement each other; a colorful meal is usually a more interesting one, though it is now quite fashionable to chose a single color theme, such as white or green for the whole meal.

Hot desserts are always appreciated more in the winter than in the summer, but even a cold summer lunch would benefit from a light hot dessert such as a soufflé, or flambéed apples; hot fruit pies can be warming without being heavy. Cold desserts are very acceptable in summer or winter, particularly when they follow heavier main courses. They also have the advantage of needing little or no last minute attention.

Serve a cheese platter before the dessert to stimulate the appetite and enable the last drop of wine to be drunk before the dessert. Once the palate has savored something sweet, wine will seem very sour tasting, unless it is a sweet one such as a sauterne.

These are the guidelines, but the final choice is, of course a personal one.

Cakes and Pastries

IN EUROPE, cakes have their origins long before Christian times, when disk-shaped cakes were made to celebrate the Midsummer Solstice, the shape being like the sun. For centuries since Christian times, cakes have been baked for symbolic reasons to celebrate important days in the Christian calendar, with every country having its own specialties. The French celebrate the feast of Epiphany by baking a simple flat round cake called a Galette, or Twelfth Night Cake. It is from these simple beginnings that more elaborate cakes have developed.

No birthday, christening, or marriage would be complete without a special cake being made to celebrate the occasion, the cake nearly always being the centerpiece of the buffet table. In Germany, a birthday is celebrated with a family gathering, seated around a table laden with torte. They remain seated for hours, eating cake and drinking coffee, and a few schnaps too! Cakes have long been associated with conviviality, happy times and friendship. They are always made for sharing with others.

All over western Europe one can see konditorei and pâtisseries displaying torte, or pastries, that are second to none anywhere in the world. Austria and Germany are particularly famous for their torte, the most famous being Vienna's Sachertorte, which was invented by Franz Sacher to satisfy the sweet tooth of Prince Klemens von Metternich, a famous statesman. From the Black Forest, Germany has given us Schwarzwalder Kirschtorte, a rich chocolate cake made with Morello cherries and cherry liqueur.

France is famous for its pastries, the lightest and richest ones being made with choux pastry. The larger, elaborate sponge cakes with mousse-like fillings are native to Austria and Germany. The famous named cakes are just the tip of the iceberg; all over Europe there are thousands more, sadly, known only to a privileged few.

Coffee and cake is a way of life to the Austrians, Germans and Swiss. Every coffee house has its own beautiful array. They are meeting houses for friends and families, particularly on a Sunday afternoon, where they can linger over a coffee and a huge slice of torte, usually topped with whipped cream, to gossip and to exchange their news.

PISTACHIO AND HAZELNUT GALETTE (page 16)

Linzertorte

Linzertorte, another Austrian specialty, is really more of a jam tart than a cake. However one classifies Linzertorte, it is a delicious and quickly made dessert. The pastry acquires its distinctive coloring from the fact that the almonds are ground with their skins on. Linzertorte is best eaten when it has cooled to room temperature, but is still excellent cold.

1¾ cups flour
1¼ cups unblanched
  almonds, ground finely
pinch of salt
1 teaspoon freshly ground
  cinnamon
1½ cups confectioners'
  sugar, sifted
finely grated rind of
  1 lemon
½ lb (2 sticks) unsalted
  butter, at room
  temperature
2 large egg yolks
1 cup raspberry jam

Glaze
1 small egg, beaten with
  1 tablespoon milk
1 tablespoon milk
1 teaspoon sugar

Decoration
2 tablespoons (½ oz)
  sliced almonds,
  optional
confectioners' sugar for
  sifting

SERVES TWELVE TO SIXTEEN

Mix the flour, almonds, salt, cinnamon, confectioners' sugar and lemon rind in a bowl. Cut the butter into pieces and add to the mixture with the egg yolks. Work all the ingredients together until they form a smooth ball of pastry. Wrap in plastic wrap and chill for about 40 minutes, until the pastry is firm.

Place a square of foil on a baking sheet, then place an 11-inch diameter 1¼-inch deep flan ring in the center. Butter the ring, then bring the foil up smoothly around the side of the ring to seal the bottom edge and prevent the pastry seeping out at the beginning of baking.

Roll out just a little more than half of the pastry on a lightly floured surface to a round 1 inch larger than the flan ring. Line the flan ring with the pastry, pressing it smoothly around the side. Trim the pastry level with the top of the flan ring.

Add the pastry trimmings to the remaining pastry and roll out to an oblong about 11×6 inches, the same thickness as the pastry in the flan ring. Trim the edges neatly, then cut into 10 long strips, about ½ inch wide.

Spread the raspberry jam evenly over the bottom of the pastry in the flan ring. Lay the pastry strips flat on top of the jam (the sides of the pastry will be above them) in a lattice pattern, cutting them to fit exactly. Loosen the sides of the pastry from the flan ring with a small narrow spatula, then bring them down over the pastry strips to form a neat border.

Lightly whisk the egg, milk, and sugar for the glaze together, then brush evenly over the pastry. Sprinkle the torte with sliced almonds, if wished. Bake in a preheated 400° oven for 10 minutes, then reduce the oven temperature to 350° and continue cooking for 35 minutes until the pastry is golden brown. Allow to cool on the baking sheet without removing the flan ring.

When the pastry begins to firm up, run a narrow spatula carefully around the sides to loosen the flan ring – but do not remove the ring until the torte has cooled to room temperature.

Remove the flan ring, sift the confectioners' sugar over the torte and transfer to a doily-lined plate.

Pithiviers

This decorative puff pastry cake is a specialty of Pithiviers, a town just south of Paris. It is filled with a rum-flavored almond cream, and the top is scored in a distinctive spiral pattern.

1 quantity of puff pastry (see page 89)	¾ cup (4oz) ground almonds
Filling	*Glaze*
4 tablespoons unsalted butter	1 egg
1½ cups confectioners' sugar, sifted	2 teaspoons confectioners' sugar, sifted
2 egg yolks	
2 tablespoons rum	SERVES EIGHT

Cut the pastry into two equal pieces. Roll out each piece on a lightly floured surface to a square, a little larger than 10 inches. Cut a 10-inch round from each piece of pastry, using a large plate or saucepan lid as a guide. Place one of the rounds on a baking sheet.

Beat the butter until very soft, then beat in the confectioners' sugar, egg yolks and rum. Mix in the ground almonds until well combined.

Spread the almond filling in the center of the pastry round on the baking sheet, leaving a border of about 1 inch all around. Brush the pastry border with a little cold water, then place the second pastry round on top to enclose the filling. Press the edges firmly together to seal. Chill the pastry for at least 30 minutes.

Make the glaze by lightly beating the egg and the confectioners' sugar together. Lightly flake the edge of the pastry by tapping it gently with a small knife, then decorate the edge by fluting it all the way round with the back of a knife.

Brush the top of the pastry with beaten egg glaze – do not allow the glaze to run down the side of the pastry as this will prevent it rising evenly. Using a small sharp knife, mark the top of the pastry with long curved lines, scoring about halfway through the pastry, starting at the center of the pastry and ending at the edge. The lines should be about ¼ inch apart and should look like a spiral pattern when finished. Make a small hole in the center to allow the steam to escape.

Bake in a preheated 450° oven for about 20–25 minutes until well risen and golden brown. Remove from the oven and cool on the baking sheet. Serve when the pastry has cooled to room temperature.

Chocolate Eclairs

Most of the eclairs sold in pâtisseries in France are filled with crème pâtissière, either vanilla, chocolate, or coffee flavored and are iced with chocolate or fondant icing. They may also be glazed with caramel.

1 quantity of choux pastry (see page 91)
1 quantity of crème pâtissière (see page 93) with 2½ oz semi-sweet chocolate melted with the milk

Icing
4 oz semi-sweet chocolate, broken into small pieces
2 tablespoons water
2 tablespoons unsalted butter

MAKES TWENTY-TWO

Line two large baking sheets with baking parchment paper cutting it to fit neatly.

Put the choux pastry into a pastry bag fitted with a ½-inch plain tip. Pipe the choux pastry onto the lined baking sheets in short straight lines, 3½ inches long, cutting the choux pastry cleanly away from the tip at the end of each line with a small knife. Bake in a preheated 425° oven for 25–30 minutes until well risen, golden brown and crisp. Remove from the oven and pierce each eclair at one end to allow the steam to escape. Return to the oven for 5 minutes to dry out completely. Transfer to a wire rack to cool.

Put the crème pâtissière into a pastry bag fitted with a ¼-inch plain tip and pipe the cream into each eclair through the hole made in the end. As you pipe the cream into the eclairs, shake them gently to make sure that the cream goes right to the bottom.

To make the icing, put the chocolate in a deep plate with the water. Place the plate over a saucepan of hot water until the chocolate melts, stirring until smooth. Remove from the heat and gradually stir in the butter.

Dip the top of each eclair in the chocolate, then place on a wire rack and put in a cool place or refrigerate until set.

Mille-Feuille

Translated, mille-feuille means a thousand leaves. Mille-feuille is made up of layers of puff pastry sandwiched together with crème pâtissière. Classic mille-feuille is made up of round layers of pastry, but it can also be made with oblong layers, which are easier to handle.

1 quantity of puff pastry (see page 89)
1 quantity of crème pâtissière (see page 93)
3 tablespoons raspberry jam
2¼ cups confectioners' sugar, sifted

2 tablespoons boiling water
⅓ cup (1½ oz) blanched, toasted and finely chopped almonds

SERVES EIGHT

Roll out the puff pastry on a lightly floured surface to an oblong, 13×15 inches. Trim the pastry edges neatly, then prick the pastry well with a fork. Cut into three oblongs, each one 5×13 inches. Place the pastry strips on baking sheets and chill for 30 minutes.

Dampen the baking sheets around the pastry strips with a little cold water. Bake in a preheated 450° oven for 25–30 minutes until well risen and golden brown. Cool the pastry strips on a wire rack.

Place the puff pastry layers one on top of the

other and trim the sides neatly. Choose the most even layer for the top, turning it upside down if necessary to make a flat surface.

Place the bottom layer on a serving dish and spread with half of the crème pâtissière and jam. Place the second pastry layer on top and spread with the remaining jam and crème pâtissière, then place the last layer of pastry on top with the flat side uppermost.

Mix the confectioners' sugar with the hot water to form an icing thick enough to coat the back of the spoon – do not make it too thin. Spread the icing evenly over the top layer of pastry and immediately sprinkle it with the chopped almonds. Allow the icing to set. Serve cut into slices.

Religieuse

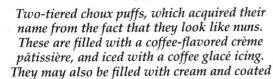

Two-tiered choux puffs, which acquired their name from the fact that they look like nuns. These are filled with a coffee-flavored crème pâtissière, and iced with a coffee glacé icing. They may also be filled with cream and coated with chocolate icing, if preferred.

1 quantity of choux pastry (see page 91)
1½ quantities of crème pâtissière (see page 93) with 1 tablespoon instant coffee added to the milk when making the custard
½ quantity of crème Chantilly (see page 94)

Icing
3 cups confectioners' sugar, sifted
1 teaspoon instant coffee
3 tablespoons boiling water

MAKES TWELVE

Line several baking sheets with baking parchment paper. Put the choux pastry into a pastry bag fitted with a ½-inch plain tip. Pipe 12 buns, 2 inches in diameter, onto the baking sheets, spacing them well apart. Then pipe another 12 smaller buns, about 1½ inches in diameter. Bake the buns, with the small ones placed below the larger ones, in a preheated 425° oven for about 35 minutes until they are well risen, golden brown and crisp. Remove from the oven and pierce underneath to allow the steam to escape. Return the buns to the oven for 5 minutes to dry out completely. Transfer to a wire rack to cool.

Put the coffee-flavored crème pâtissière into a pastry bag fitted with a ¼-inch plain tip. Fill all the buns with the crème pâtissière, piping it in through the hole made in the bottom. Place the buns, spaced well apart, on a wire rack. Place the rack over a tray or large plate.

To make the icing, put the confectioners' sugar into a bowl and make a well in the center. Dissolve the coffee granules in the boiling water, then add to the sugar and mix together to form a smooth, shiny icing that will coat the back of the spoon. Spoon the icing evenly over each choux bun, then leave until completely set before fitting together.

Whip the crème Chantilly until thick enough to pipe, then fill a pastry bag fitted with a large star tip. Pipe a rosette on top of each large choux bun, then carefully place the smaller buns on top of the cream, pressing gently into the cream to secure.

Schwarzwalder Kirschtorte
(Black Forest Cherry Cake)

This famous, and much loved, cake from the Black Forest is perfect for any grand occasion, or as a dessert for a dinner party. The cherries should really be fresh Morello cherries, but as these are not always easy to come by, canned cherries can be used instead. When fresh Morello cherries are available, poach them in a sugar syrup and remove their pits. The following recipe is a very lavish version.

Chocolate Génoise
7 eggs
1 cup sugar
¾ cup cake flour
¾ cup cocoa
7 tablespoons unsalted
   butter, melted and
   cooled

Filling
two 16-oz cans pitted
   dark cherries
1 cup granulated sugar
7 tablespoons Kirsch

4 cups heavy cream
2 tablespoons
   confectioners' sugar,
   sifted

Decoration
6 oz semi-sweet chocolate
   at room temperature
12 fresh cherries with
   stems

SERVES TWELVE

Make the chocolate Génoise as instructed on page 86, sifting the flour and cocoa together twice before adding to the egg mixture. Bake the sponge cake in a preheated 350° oven for 35–40 minutes.

Make the chocolate decoration. Line a baking sheet with wax paper, then working directly over the paper, pull a potato peeler along the edge of the chocolate, not the flat surface, to form a curl.

Continue until the chocolate is used up. Chill the chocolate curls until needed.

Make the filling: drain the cherries, reserving 1¼ cups of their juice. Put the cherry juice into a saucepan with the granulated sugar. Heat gently until the sugar dissolves, then boil the syrup until it reduces by about half and is thickened. Allow to cool, then stir in 3 tablespoons Kirsch. Whip half of the cream with 2 tablespoons Kirsch and 1 tablespoon confectioners' sugar.

Cut the chocolate sponge into three layers. Cut a piece of cardboard the same size as the sponge cake. Place the cardboard on the work surface, then place the bottom layer of sponge on the cardboard. Fit a torten ring around the sponge cake, snugly but not too tightly. Or, cut a strip of thin cardboard long enough to fit around the sponge cake and 2½ inches deep. Secure the cardboard firmly in position with tape.

Brush the cherry syrup all over the layer of sponge cake to moisten it well. Spread with half the whipped cream, then arrange half the cherries on top. Place the second layer of sponge cake on top of the cherries, and moisten well with more cherry syrup. Spread with the remaining whipped cream, and cover with the remaining cherries. Brush the underside of the top layer of sponge with cherry syrup and place it, syrup-side down, on top of the cherries. Press the cake firmly together.

Whip the remaining cream with the remaining Kirsch and confectioners' sugar. Spread a layer of cream over the top of the cake. Remove the torten ring, or the cardboard, from around the cake.

Spread the side of the cake with a smooth layer of cream, then coat the sides evenly with the chocolate curls – the piece of cardboard under the cake will make it easy to pick the cake up for this process.

Place the cake on a serving plate, and mark the top into 12 equal sections. Whip the remaining cream until it is thick enough to pipe, then fill a pastry bag fitted with a medium-sized star tip.

Working from the center of the cake out, pipe a large shell of cream in each section on top of the cake, then pipe a star of cream where each shell finishes. Sprinkle any remaining chocolate curls over the top of the cake, then, decorate the stars with the fresh cherries. Keep the cake in a cool place until ready to serve.

Paris-Brest

This specialty of Paris is a large choux ring, split and filled with praline-flavored cream. It could also be filled with crème Chantilly and fresh fruits, such as strawberries and raspberries. The top is strewn with sliced almonds, giving it a very attractive appearance.

1 quantity of choux pastry (see page 91)	⅔ cup sugar
	8 ladyfingers
⅓ cup (1 oz) almonds blanched and cut into fine slivers	3–4 tablespoons Grand Marnier
	2½ cups heavy cream confectioners' sugar for sifting
Filling	
¾ cup (4 oz) unblanched almonds	SERVES EIGHT TO TEN

Line a large baking sheet with baking parchment paper, then draw an 8 inch circle on the paper, using a plate as a guide.

Put the choux pastry into a large pastry bag fitted with a large star tip. Following the drawn circle, pipe two rings of choux close together on the baking sheet, then pipe two more rings on the top. Scatter the slivered almonds evenly over the top, then bake in a preheated 425° oven for 40–45 minutes until well risen and crispy. Remove the choux ring from the oven and pierce it in several places to allow the steam to escape. Return to the oven for 5–10 minutes to dry out completely.

Transfer the choux ring to a wire rack and allow to cool for a few minutes, then slice horizontally in half, cutting evenly around the center. Separate the two halves, then scoop out any uncooked pastry from the center. Allow to cool completely.

To make the filling, put the unblanched almonds and sugar into a heavy-based saucepan and heat very gently until the sugar dissolves and turns a rich caramel color – do not let it become too dark as this will make the praline bitter. Pour the nuts onto a lightly oiled baking sheet, allow to cool, then finely crush or grind.

Cut the ladyfingers in half and lay them in a shallow dish. Sprinkle the Grand Marnier over them, cover and leave to stand until the ladyfingers have absorbed the liqueur.

Whip the cream until it just holds its shape, then carefully fold in the praline.

Place the bottom half of the choux ring on a plate and fill with half the praline cream. Break up the soaked ladyfingers with a fork, then spoon over the praline cream. Spread the remaining praline cream evenly on top of the ladyfingers. Replace the top of the choux ring, then sift lightly with confectioners' sugar. Chill until ready to serve.

Pistachio and Hazelnut Galette

This simple cake is made with two rounds of pistachio and hazelnut pastry, filled with a Grand Marnier-flavored cream, mangoes and mandarin orange segments.

1⅓ cups cake flour
pinch of salt
¾ cup confectioners' sugar
½ cup (2 oz) pistachio nuts, skinned and ground fairly finely
¼ cup (1 oz) hazelnuts, skinned, toasted, and ground fairly finely
14 tablespoons unsalted butter, cut into pieces

Filling
2½ cups heavy double cream

finely grated rind of 1 orange
2 tablespoons Grand Marnier
1 tablespoon confectioners' sugar
1 large ripe mango
16-oz mandarin orange segments
confectioners' sugar for sifting
chopped pistachio nuts for sprinkling

SERVES TWELVE

Sift the flour, salt and confectioners' sugar into a bowl, add the nuts and mix well together. Rub the butter into the flour and nut mixture, working the ingredients together gently until they form a ball.

Cut the pastry into two equal pieces, roll out each piece on a lightly floured surface to a round a little smaller than 10 inches. Place each pastry round in a 10-inch fluted tart pan, then press the pastry gently over the bottom of the pans until it fits exactly – smooth the pastry with the back of a spoon, but do not stretch it.

Prick with a fork, and bake in a preheated 350° oven for 20–25 minutes until the pastry is cooked and very lightly browned (if you have only one tart pan, bake the pastry rounds one at a time, keeping the one not being baked refrigerated until needed). Remove the cooked pastry rounds from the oven and immediately cut one of the rounds into 12 triangular-shaped pieces. Allow to cool slightly, then transfer to wire racks to cool completely.

Whip the cream with the orange rind, Grand Marnier and confectioners' sugar until it will hold soft peaks. Peel the mango, then cut the flesh from the seed in long thin slices. Drain the orange segments well, putting about 12 of the best ones aside for decoration.

Carefully place the whole pastry round on a large plate. Spread a generous layer of cream over the pastry, then arrange the mango slices and orange segments evenly over the cream.

Whip remaining cream until thick enough to pipe and fill a pastry bag fitted with a large star tip. Pipe 12 large rosettes on top of the fruits, about 1 inch in from the edge. Arrange the triangular-shaped pieces of pastry on top of the galette, placing them at an angle, each one supported by a rosette of cream. Sift confectioners' sugar lightly over the galette. Decorate the galette with the remaining cream and reserved mandarin orange segments and sprinkle over the nuts.

GÂTEAU SAINT-HONORÉ (page 18)

Jalousie

A simple puff pastry cake filled with raspberry jam, perfect for afternoon tea, or to have with coffee.

---

1 quantity of puff pastry (see page 89)	1 small egg, beaten with 2 teaspoons sifted confectioners' sugar
⅔ cup raspberry jam	confectioners' sugar for sifting

SERVES EIGHT

Roll out the puff pastry on a lightly floured surface to a square a little larger than 12 inches. Trim the pastry edges to form an exact 12-inch square. Cut the pastry equally in half. Place the pastry lengths on baking sheets and chill for about 10 minutes. Chilling the pastry at this stage will make it much easier to assemble.

Spread the raspberry jam down the center of one of the pieces of pastry, leaving a 1-inch border all around.

Remove the second piece of pastry from the baking sheet and fold in half lengthwise, then make cuts all along the folded edge to within 1 inch of the edges, spacing the cuts about ½ inch apart. Without unfolding the pastry, place it on top of the pastry spread with jam so that the edges line up with the bottom piece of pastry, then carefully unfold the pastry to cover the jam completely. Press all the pastry edges well together to seal. Chill for 30 minutes.

Remove the chilled jalousie from the refrigerator, then flake the edge with a small knife and mark into flutes. Brush the top with the beaten egg – do not

allow the glaze to run down the sides as it will prevent them from rising. Bake in a preheated 450° oven for 20–30 minutes until it is well risen, and golden brown. Allow to cool. Sift with confectioners' sugar then place on a doily-lined tray. To serve, cut into slices across the jalousie.

Gâteau Saint-Honoré

This pastry is named after Saint-Honoré, who was a Bishop of Amiens and is considered the patron saint of bakers. It is a wonderful cake, that combines two types of pastry, pâte sucrée and choux, to form a case that may be filled with an endless variety of fillings. This recipe uses the traditional crème Saint-Honoré, topped with a chocolate-flavored cream.

---

1 quantity of pâte sucrée (see page 92)	*Caramel*
	1⅓ cups sugar
1 quantity of choux pastry (see page 91)	6 tablespoons water
Crème Saint-Honoré	*Topping*
double quantity of ingredients for crème pâtissière (see page 93)	3 oz semi-sweet chocolate, broken into small pieces
1 tablespoon unflavored gelatin	3 tablespoons water
3 tablespoons water	1¼ cups heavy double cream
2 tablespoons Grand Marnier	chopped pistachio nuts for sprinkling

SERVES TWELVE

Roll out the pâte sucrèe on a flat, or upturned, baking sheet to a round a little larger than 11 inches in diameter. Using a flan ring or saucepan lid as a guide, cut the pastry into an 11-inch round. Remove the trimmings, then prick the pastry all over with a fork. Chill for 30 minutes.

Put the choux pastry into a pastry bag fitted with a ½ inch plain tip. Pipe a single ring of choux pastry around the edge of the pâte sucrée, about ¼ inch in from the edge. Bake in a preheated 400° oven for 25–30 minutes until the choux pastry is well risen, golden brown and crisp. Remove from the oven and pierce the choux ring at intervals to allow the steam to escape. Return to the oven for 2–3 minutes to dry out completely. Transfer to a wire rack to cool.

Meanwhile, line a large baking sheet with baking parchment paper and pipe the remaining choux pastry in whirls, about 1½ inches in diameter, on the baking sheet, spacing them well apart (only 14–15 buns are needed for the gâteau but it is best to make extra buns because all those used have to be perfect). Bake in a preheated 425° oven for 25–30 minutes until well risen, golden brown and crisp. Remove from the oven and pierce each bun underneath to allow the steam to escape. Return to the oven for about 5 minutes to dry out completely. Transfer to a wire rack to cool.

To make the crème Saint-Honoré, prepare the crème pâtissière to the stage where the custard is cooled, ready for adding the egg whites and cream. Dissolve the gelatin in the water in a small bowl. Beat the egg whites until stiff, then fold into the cooled custard. Whip the cream, adding the Grand Marnier, until it just holds its shape, then quickly whisk in the gelatin. Fold the cream into the custard. Keep at room temperature while completing the gâteau.

Spoon some of the crème Saint-Honoré into a pastry bag fitted with a ¼-inch plain tip, and fill 14–15 of the best choux buns, piping it in through the hole made in the bottom. Scrape any cream from the base of the buns with a small spatula. Put the buns aside while making the caramel.

To make the caramel, put the sugar into a saucepan with the water and heat gently until the sugar has dissolved, brushing down the sides of the saucepan with the hot water from time to time. Bring the syrup to a boil and boil until it turns a golden caramel color. Immediately, plunge the base of the saucepan into cold water to prevent the caramel darkening further. Place the saucepan in a large bowl and fill the bowl to halfway up the side of the saucepan with boiling water – this will keep the caramel fluid.

Place the pâte sucrée base on a plate. Take one of the choux buns and dip the base in the caramel, then place it on the choux ring, holding it in position for a few seconds to secure. Continue with the remaining buns, placing them close together. Spoon the remaining caramel over each bun to coat evenly. Spoon the remaining crème Saint-Honoré into the choux case. Chill while making the topping.

Put the chocolate into a small bowl with the water. Place the bowl over a pan of hot water until the chocolate melts, stirring frequently until smooth. Remove from the heat and allow to cool. Whip the cream until thick but not buttery, then carefully fold in the cooled chocolate.

Put the chocolate cream into a pastry bag fitted with a medium-sized star tip and pipe the cream decoratively over the top of a the crème Saint-Honoré. Sprinkle with pistachio nuts and serve. If not serving immediately, keep in a cool place – the gâteau will stand quite well for 1–2 hours.

Raspberry Torte

This rich, creamy cake is very like the many elaborate torte one finds across Europe – they don't have famous names, but are the proud creations of individual cafés and pâtisseries. This one is made with a raspberry-flavored bavarois mixture, generously decorated with cream and fresh raspberries.

Génoise
4 eggs
⅔ cup sugar
¾ cup cake flour, sifted
4 tablespoons unsalted butter, melted and cooled

Pastry base
1 quantity of pâte sucrée (see page 92)
1 tablespoon seedless raspberry jelly

Bavarois
4 egg yolks
3 tablespoons sugar
1 cup milk
4 teaspoons unflavored gelatin
1¼ cups heavy cream
2 tablespoons confectioners' sugar, sifted
½ lb fresh raspberries, sieved

Topping
1½ teaspoons unflavored gelatin
2 tablespoons water
1¼ cups heavy cream
1 tablespoon confectioners' sugar, sifted
1 tablespoon Kirsch

Decoration
1¼ cups heavy cream
½ cup (2 oz) slivered almonds, lightly toasted
fresh raspberries

SERVES TWELVE

Make the Génoise as instructed on page 86, baking it in a 10-inch springform pan.

Roll the pâte sucrée out on a flat, or upturned baking sheet to a round a little larger than 10 inches. Cut the pastry to a neat 10-inch round, using a large plate as a guide. Remove the trimmings, then prick the pastry well all over with a fork. Chill for 30 minutes, then bake in a preheated 400° oven for 15–20 minutes until very lightly browned.

To make the raspberry bavarois, lightly beat the egg yolks and the sugar together. Heat the milk until almost boiling, then beat it into the egg yolks. Cook over a pan of hot water until the custard is thick enough to coat the back of the spoon evenly (or, cook in a microwave oven on full power, for 2–2½ minutes, stirring every 30 seconds with a wire whisk).

Immediately the custard thickens, pour it through a nylon sieve into a clean bowl. Add the gelatin and stir until dissolved. Allow to cool, stirring frequently to prevent a skin forming.

Whip the cream with the confectioners' sugar until it will hold soft peaks. Mix the cooked custard and the raspberry purée together until well blended, then fold in the cream. Cut the sponge into two equal layers, trimming the top edge to level.

Place the pâte sucrée base on a plate, then spread evenly with the raspberry jelly. Place the bottom layer of sponge on top of the jelly. Trim the pastry base to exactly the same size as the sponge. Place a torten ring around the pastry and sponge to fit snugly, but not too tightly. (If you do not have a torten ring – cut a length of flexible cardboard long enough to fit around the pastry, and about 3 inches deep. Secure the cardboard with tape.)

Pour the raspberry bavarois mixture on top of the sponge, then chill until beginning to set. Place the top layer of sponge on top and chill until very firm.

To make the topping, dissolve the gelatin in ☞

RASPBERRY TORTE (above)

the water in a small bowl. Whip the cream with the confectioners' sugar and Kirsch until it will just hold its shape, then quickly whisk in the gelatin. Pour the cream over the top sponge and spread evenly. Chill until set.

To decorate, remove the torten ring or cardboard. Whip the cream until it just holds its shape. Spread the sides of the torte with some of the cream, then coat evenly with sliced almonds. Whip the remaining cream until thick enough to pipe and fill a pastry bag fitted with a medium-sized star tip.

Mark the top of the torte into 12. Starting at the outside edge and working to center, pipe a curved scroll in each section. Decorate with raspberries.

Palmiers

The pastry for these Parisian specialties is folded and cut in such a way that they look like hearts. These palmiers are filled with fresh strawberries and a strawberry cream, but they can be filled with crème Chantilly alone. As a special treat, use wild strawberries when they are available.

1 quantity of puff pastry (see page 89)	2 teaspoons confectioners' sugar sifted
⅔ cup sugar	1 lb fresh strawberries, hulled
2 teaspoons apple pie spice	confectioners' sugar for sifting
a little milk for brushing	
1 cup heavy cream	MAKES TEN
2 tablespoons strawberry purée	

Roll out the puff pastry on a lightly floured surface to an oblong, about 19×21 inches. Trim the edges neatly.

Mix the sugar and the spice together. Brush the pastry very lightly with a little milk, then sprinkle lightly with some of the sugar and spice. Fold the two longest sides to the center of the pastry, to meet. Brush the pastry with a little more milk and sprinkle with more sugar and spice. Fold the long, folded sides, to the center again. Brush the pastry with a little more milk and sprinkle with the remaining sugar and spice. Fold the two folded sides together.

Cut the pastry strip into twenty 1-inch wide pieces. Take one of the pastry pieces and turn it onto its side on a lightly floured surface, flatten slightly with the palm of your hand, then roll it out gently on a baking sheet to about 4 inches long, then repeat with the remaining pieces. Refrigerate the palmiers for about 30 minutes.

Brush each palmier with a little milk to glaze, then bake in a preheated 450° oven for 20–25 minutes until they are golden brown and cooked. Transfer immediately to a wire rack to cool.

Whip the cream with the strawberry purée and confectioners' sugar until thick enough to pipe and fill a pastry bag fitted with a large star tip. Pipe the cream on 10 of the pastry hearts. If the strawberries are very large, cut them into slices; if they are small, cut each one in half. Leave wild strawberries whole.

Arrange the strawberries on top of the cream, then place the remaining pastry hearts on top of the strawberries, placing them at a slight angle. Sift confectioners' sugar lightly over the palmiers and serve.

Sachertorte

*Famous the world over, Sachertorte was the
invention of Franz Sacher, a master sugar baker,
in Vienna in 1832. It is a very rich, moist,
chocolate cake served, more often than not, with
whipped cream. There are many versions of
Sachertorte: some are made with an apricot jam
filling, some are made without.*

*The traditional Sachertorte is covered with a
chocolate fondant icing, but as this can be
rather sweet, a ganache icing is used here. This
icing is extremely simple to make and use. It
sets with a high gloss, contrasting perfectly
with the moist cake inside, both in texture and
flavor. Sachertorte is not normally decorated; it
looks superb in its simplicity.*

---

6 oz semi-sweet chocolate
12 tablespoons (1½ sticks)
   unsalted butter
⅔ cup sugar
1 teaspoon vanilla extract
6 egg yolks
6 egg whites
1¼ cups (6 oz) ground
   almonds
6 tablespoons potato flour

apricot glaze made with
   ⅔ cup apricot jam (see
   page 94)

Icing
8 oz semi-sweet
   chocolate, broken into
   small pieces
1 cup heavy double cream

SERVES SIXTEEN

Thoroughly butter a 10-inch round springform pan,
then line the bottom with non-stick baking
parchment paper. Lightly dust the sides with flour.

Break the chocolate into small pieces, put into a
small bowl over a saucepan of hot water and heat
until the chocolate melts. Stir until smooth. Beat the
butter with half the sugar and the vanilla extract
until light and fluffy. Gradually beat in the egg
yolks, and then the melted chocolate.

Beat the egg whites until stiff, but not dry, then
gradually beat in the remaining sugar. Fold the egg
whites into the chocolate mixture, alternately with
the ground almonds and potato flour. Spoon the
mixture into the prepared pan and bake in a
preheated 350° oven for 40–45 minutes, until a
toothpick or wooden skewer inserted into the center
comes out clean. Allow the cake to cool in the pan.

Carefully remove the cake from the pan, turn it
upside down and remove the baking paper. Slice the
cake into two equal layers. Heat the apricot glaze
until boiling. Place the bottom layer of cake on a
wire rack. Spread apricot glaze all over the cake
layer, then place the second layer on top, pressing
the two firmly together. Re-boil the apricot glaze and
brush it evenly all over the cake until well coated.
Allow to set. Place the cake on the rack over a large
plate to ice it.

Make the icing: put the chocolate and cream into a
pan and heat gently until the chocolate melts and
blends smoothly with cream – do not allow to boil.
Remove from the heat and stir gently to cool just a
little. Pour the chocolate cream, all at once, onto the
center of the cake and allow it to run over the top
and down the sides to coat the cake completely. If
necessary, ease the cream over the cake with a long
narrow spatula. Tap the rack gently to level the
cream. Leave in a cool place, not the refrigerator,
until the chocolate cream sets firmly. Serve the
Sachertorte on a doily-lined plate.

Dobostorte

This cake, of Hungarian origin, is fascinating to make, but may be a little bewildering the first time you do so. It is made up of thin layers of fatless sponge mixture sandwiched together with chocolate butter cream. The top is glazed with caramel and the whole thing looks quite wonderful when completed. You don't need a special pan to bake it in, but you do need several baking sheets.

8 eggs	1 teaspoon vanilla extract
1 cup sugar	½ cup + 2 tablespoons
1¾ cups cake flour, sifted	cocoa, sifted
	2 tablespoons brandy,
Buttercream	optional
8 egg yolks	
2 cups sugar	*Caramel*
¾ cup water	1 cup sugar
1 lb (4 sticks) unsalted	5 tablespoons water
butter	
	SERVES TWELVE

Cut six sheets of baking parchment paper, about 11 inches square. Draw a 10-inch circle on each sheet of paper. Line as many baking sheets as you have with the paper. The sponge layers will have to be cooked in relays, depending on the number of shelves you have in your oven. It is a simple process to reline the sheets.

To make the sponge layers, beat the eggs and sugar in a bowl placed over a pan of hot water until pale and thick. Remove from the heat and continue whisking until cool, and the mixture holds the trail of a beater. Gradually fold in the flour.

Put 2–3 tablespoons of the mixture into the center of the drawn circles, then spread evenly with a long narrow spatula to form thin layers. Bake the sponge layers, in batches, in a preheated 425° oven for 6–7 minutes until they are lightly risen and firm to the touch. Remove from the oven and allow to cool.

To make the buttercream, beat the egg yolks until very thick. Put the sugar into a saucepan with the water and heat gently until the sugar has dissolved, brushing down the sides of the pan with hot water. Boil the syrup until it reaches a temperature of 240° on a candy thermometer, when a little of the syrup dropped into cold water forms a soft ball.

Beat the syrup, in a thin stream, into the egg yolks. Continue to beat until the mixture cools and thickens. Beat the butter until it is very light and fluffy, then beat in the vanilla, cocoa and brandy if using. Gradually beat the egg yolk mixture into the butter, a little at a time.

Carefully remove the sponge layers from the baking paper. Trim one of the sponges to form a neat round – cutting it to the largest round possible. Lightly butter a sheet of foil, then place the sponge layer on it. Thoroughly butter a long narrow spatula and a metal ruler.

To make the caramel, put the sugar into a pan with the water and heat gently until the sugar has dissolved, brushing down the sides of the pan. Boil the syrup until it turns a rich caramel color – not too dark. Immediately, pour the caramel onto the center of the sponge cake on the foil, then spread it out evenly with the buttered spatula. Working quite quickly, mark the caramel equally into 12 with the buttered ruler by pressing down gently but firmly on the caramel, and buttering the edge of the ruler each time you make an indentation. Allow the caramel to set.

Meanwhile, on a flat baking sheet, sandwich all the remaining layers of sponge together, without ☞

SHERBETS (pages 34 and 35)

trimming them, with generous layers of chocolate buttercream, ending with a layer of buttercream spread very evenly. Place the caramel coated layer of sponge on the top. Trim around the sides of the sponge layers, to level with the caramel coated layer.

Spread a good layer of buttercream around the sides of the torte, without letting it spoil the caramel coated layer, spreading it as smoothly as possible. Using a serrated cake scraper, mark the side of the torte with continuous lines – placing the torte on a turntable will make this job easier. Chill for about 30 minutes. Serve on a doily-lined plate. Cut into wedges by cutting through the caramel topping at the indentations.

Nusskuchen

Nusskuchen comes in many forms, but is always made with nuts of some kind. This is a light biscuit de Savoie sponge filled with a hazelnut buttercream.

1 biscuit de Savoie sponge cake (see page 87)	½ lb (2 sticks) unsalted butter
2 cups (9 oz) hazelnuts	1 teaspoon vanilla extract
Buttercream	SERVES TWELVE
4 egg whites	
3 cups confectioners' sugar, sifted	

Make the biscuit de Savoie sponge as instructed and allow to cool.

Put the hazelnuts on a baking sheet, then bake in a preheated 350° oven for 10–15 minutes until their skins become loose. Put the nuts in a clean dish towel and rub until the skins are removed. Put the skinned nuts on the baking sheet and return to the oven for 5–10 minutes until lightly browned. Remove from the oven and allow to cool. Put about 24 nuts aside for decoration, then chop the rest finely.

To make the buttercream, put the egg whites and confectioners' sugar in a large bowl placed over a pan of hot water, then beat until they form a stiff shiny meringue – do not allow the meringue to become too hot. Remove from the heat and continue beating until the meringue is cooled, and will form stiff peaks.

Beat the butter until it is very light and fluffy, then beat in the vanilla extract. Gradually beat the meringue into the butter then divide the buttercream in two and mix half the chopped nuts into one half.

Slice the sponge cake into three equal layers. Sandwich the sponge layers together with the hazelnut buttercream. Spread plain buttercream over the top and around the sides of the sponge cake. Coat the sides with the remaining chopped hazelnuts. Place the cake on a plate.

Put the remaining buttercream into a pastry bag fitted with a small star tip. Pipe a decorative edge around the top of the cake, then decorate with the reserved whole hazelnuts. Keep in a cool place or refrigerate until ready to serve.

Danish Pastries

The Danes serve Danish pastries for breakfast, but they are perfect for serving with morning coffee, or afternoon tea. Serve freshly baked.

1 quantity of Danish
   pastry (see page 90)

Almond filling
2 tablespoons unsalted
   butter
⅓ cup sugar
1 egg yolk
⅓ cup (2 oz) ground
   almonds

Apricot filling
6 large ripe apricots,
   skinned, halved and
   pitted or, 12 canned
   apricot halves
1–2 teaspoons sugar

Spice filling
2 tablespoons butter
3 tablespoons sugar
1 teaspoon apple pie
   spice
¼ cup seedless raisins or
   currants (1½ oz)

Glazes
1 egg, beaten
1 quantity of apricot glaze
   (see page 94)

Decorations
3¼ cups confectioners'
   sugar, sifted
lemon juice
3 tablespoons chopped
   glacé cherries
3 tablespoons chopped
   candied angelica
a little hot water
2 tablespoons (½ oz)
   skinned and chopped
   pistachio nuts
1 tablespoon rum
2 tablespoons (½ oz)
   slivered almonds,
   lightly toasted

MAKES EIGHTEEN

For almond crescents, make the almond filling by beating the butter with the sugar until soft, then beat in the egg yolk and ground almonds. Roll out one-third of the pastry on a lightly floured surface to a square, a little larger than 10 inches. Cut a neat 10-inch round from the pastry, remove the trimmings, then cut the round into six triangles. Put one-quarter of the almond mixture aside and divide the rest into six.

Take one piece of dough, and place a piece of the almond mixture at the widest end. Roll the pastry up toward the point, then shape into a crescent. Place on a well greased baking sheet, with the point tucked under. Repeat with the remaining pastry, spacing the crescents well apart on the baking sheet. Cover loosely with plastic wrap.

For apricot envelopes, roll out one-third of the pastry to an oblong, 8×12 inches. Trim the edges, then cut into six 4-inch squares. Place two apricot halves in the center of each square, then place a small piece of the reserved almond mixture in each apricot. Sprinkle the apricots with sugar. Bring two opposite corners of the pastry to the center, over the apricots, until they overlap slightly, moisten the joins with a little cold water to seal. Place well apart on a well greased baking sheet. Cover loosely with plastic wrap.

For spiced pinwheels, roll out the remaining pastry to an oblong 6×14 inches. Beat the butter, sugar and spice together until soft and creamy, then spread it evenly over the pastry. Sprinkle the raisins evenly over the spice mixture. Roll the pastry up from a short end to form a wide roll. Cut the roll into six equal slices. Place the pinwheels, cut sides down, on a well greased baking sheet, spaced apart. Cover loosely with plastic wrap.

Leave the pastries in a warm place until they have doubled in size and are springy when pressed lightly with a fingertip. Brush the pastries with the beaten egg, then bake in a preheated 425° oven for 15–20 minutes, until well risen, golden brown and crisp. Transfer to wire racks and glaze and decorate while hot. Boil the apricot glaze, then brush over all the pastries to glaze evenly.

To decorate crescents, mix 1 cup of the confectioners' sugar with sufficient lemon juice to form a thin icing, then dribble the icing over the hot pastries and immediately sprinkle with the cherries and angelica.

For apricot envelopes mix 1 cup of the confectioners' sugar with a little hot water to form a thin icing. Dribble the icing over the hot pastries and sprinkle with chopped pistachio nuts.

For pinwheels, mix the remaining confectioners' sugar with the rum and just a little hot water to form a thin icing. Dribble the icing over the hot pastries and sprinkle with the slivered almonds.

Rigo Jancsi

Absolute temptation! These rich squares of chocolate cake, classic in their make-up of chocolate flavored Génoise and ganache, were named after a gypsy violinist, who was said to have broken the heart of many a princess.

Chocolate Génoise
3 eggs
½ cup sugar
½ cup flour sifted with
  2 tablespoons cocoa
3 tablespoons unsalted
  butter, melted and
  cooled

Ganache
15 oz semi-sweet
  chocolate, broken into
  small pieces
2½ cups heavy cream

3 tablespoons brandy

Icing
4 oz semi-sweet
  chocolate, broken into
  small pieces
1 tablespoon water
2 tablespoons brandy
1½ cups confectioners'
  sugar, sifted

MAKES TWENTY-FOUR
SQUARES

Grease a 9×13-inch jellyroll pan with butter. Line the bottom with wax paper. Make the Génoise as instructed on page 86 sifting the flour and and cocoa together, then spread evenly in the prepared pan.

Bake in a preheated 350° oven for 20–25 minutes until the sponge is well risen, firm to the touch and beginning to shrink away from the sides of the pan. Allow the sponge to cool in the pan.

To make the ganache, put the chocolate and the cream into a large saucepan and heat gently, stirring, until the chocolate melts and blends smoothly with the cream, without letting the mixture boil. Pour the ganache into a bowl and allow to cool until quite cold, but not set hard, stirring the cream frequently to prevent a skin forming. When cold, whip the cream with the brandy until it is very light and fluffy, taking care not to overwhip.

Cut the chocolate sponge into two equal pieces, cutting across the width. Place one piece on a flat board or baking sheet. Cut a length of cardboard, or several thicknesses of foil, long enough to fit around the sponge cake, and about 3 inches deep. Fit the cardboard snugly around the sponge, forming square corners as you do so, and secure with tape. Alternatively, place the sponge cake in a deep square cake pan, placing it against two sides of the pan, then form a false "wall" for the other side, with several thicknesses of foil.

Spoon the whipped ganache on top of the layer of chocolate sponge to a depth of about 2 inches and spread evenly, then place the second layer of sponge on top. Refrigerate for at least 1 hour.

To make the icing, put the chocolate into a small saucepan with the water, the brandy and confectioners' sugar. Stir over a gentle heat until the chcocolate melts and blends with the sugar to make a smooth icing. Spread the chocolate icing over the top layer of sponge cake and allow to set.

Carefully remove the "wall" from around the sponge cake. Cut the cake into twenty-four 1½-inch squares, using a sharp knife dipped in hot water and dried each time before cutting. Keep chilled until 20–30 minutes before serving.

ORANGES COOKED IN CARAMEL (page 38)

Croquembouche

A spectacular cake, served as a wedding cake in France, veiled in a cobweb of fine spun sugar. As the name implies, the cake has a crunchy texture from the caramel used to build tiny choux buns into a high pyramid shape.
It is best to make a croquembouche in a cool, dry atmosphere, and it should not be completed any longer than 1 hour ahead of serving. However, the choux buns, pastry base, and crème pâtissière can all be made in advance ready for last-minute assembly.

double quantity of choux
pastry (see page 91)
1 quantity of pâte sucrée
(see page 92)
2½ quantities of crème
pâtissière (see page 93),
flavored with
3 tablespoons Kirsch or
Grand Marnier

2½ cups sugar
½ cup water

SERVES TWENTY TO
TWENTY-FIVE

Line 3–4 baking sheets with baking parchment paper.

Put the choux pastry into a large pastry bag fitted with a ½-inch plain tip. Pipe about 90 small rounds of choux pastry onto the lined baking sheets, each one about 1¼ inches in diameter, and spacing well apart.

Bake in batches (putting those not being baked into the refrigerator while waiting) in a preheated 425° oven for 20–25 minutes until well risen, golden brown and crisp. Remove from the oven and pierce each one underneath to allow the steam to escape, then return to the oven for about 5 minutes to dry out. Cool on wire racks. Leave the oven on.

Roll out the pâte sucrée on a lightly floured surface to about ¼ inch thick. Place on a baking sheet and prick well all over with a fork. Using an 8-inch fluted tart pan, press the sharp edge of the pan into the pastry to cut it into a neat round, then remove the trimmings. Chill for 30 minutes, then bake for 20–25 minutes until very lightly browned. Allow to cool.

Fill a large pastry bag, fitted with a ¼-inch tip, with crème pâtissière. Fill each choux bun with cream, piping it in through the hole made in the bottom. Keep the buns neatly together. Place the pastry round on a flat cake stand.

Put the sugar and water in a heavy-based saucepan and heat gently until the sugar has dissolved, brushing down the sides of the saucepan with hot water. Bring to a boil and boil until it turns a pale caramel color. Immediately, plunge the base of the saucepan into cold water to stop the caramel cooking further. Then place the saucepan in a bowl and pour boiling water into the bowl to come about halfway up the side of the saucepan – this will keep the caramel fluid.

Take one of the choux buns and dip one side only in the caramel, then place it, on its side, on the edge of the pastry round, with the filling hole to the center. Continue until the pastry round is covered. Continue to build up layers of choux buns, making each layer slightly smaller, until all of the buns are used up and you have a high pyramid shape. If necessary, the caramel may be reheated during this process, but do not allow it to darken.

To form the veil, cover a large area of floor with newspaper, then cover the newspaper with sheets of wax paper. Stand the cake stand in the center of the paper.

If necessary, reheat the remaining caramel until it is liquid again. Holding two or three forks firmly together, dip the forks into the caramel, then lift them out and hold high until the caramel starts to form a very thin thread, then quickly wind the thread around the choux pyramid with a quick, twisting movement – almost throwing it around.

Repeat until all of the caramel has been used up and the choux pyramid is completely covered with a veil of spun sugar. Trim the caramel from around the base of the cake stand with lightly oiled kitchen scissors. Any spun sugar that has gathered in piles on the wax paper should be carefully lifted up and placed on top of the croquembouche. Serve as soon as is possible.

Fresh Fruit Desserts

OF ALL the ingredients available for making desserts, there are none more colorful, or more versatile than fresh fruits. They can easily be transformed into tantalizing desserts that few could resist.

Gone are the days when wonderful, exotic fresh fruit desserts were for the summer months only; they can now be part of our winter menus, too. Never before have we been so spoiled for choice. Modern methods of transportation make it possible to enjoy more and more varieties of exotic fruits from all over the world so that fruits like mangoes, papayas and passion fruit are now commonplace among the apples and pears.

Although we refer to fruit as being "in or out of season," this only applies to our own growing seasons. Strawberries are available in spring and summer, with a peak in April, May or June, depending on the region, but at other times of the year they may be imported from other countries, making it possible to buy them practically all year round. The same applies to other fruits.

However, there are still some that only appear for a short while, and there will always be gaps as the seasons change from one country to another, so before deciding on a fresh fruit dessert for a menu, check to see what is available.

You can never guarantee you'll be able to buy perfectly ripe fruit just when you want it, especially pears, peaches, apricots and mangoes. Buy these a few days beforehand to ensure that they will be ripe when you want to use them. Buy highly perishable fruits, such as raspberries, on the day you need them.

Firmer fruits may be lightly poached in a sugar syrup to soften them, and to bring out their hidden flavors. Most can be made into a purée, perfect for serving as a sauce, or for blending with custard and cream to make ice cream, mousses or sherbets. Fruits can be mixed and matched to make an endless variety of fresh fruit salads, sparkling gelatin molds, or even be left to linger on through into the winter months in a deep pot of rum known as a German rumtopf.

Compotes

Spring Compote

Compotes are mixtures of fruits cooked in sugar syrup, which can be served hot or cold. The syrup may be flavored with spices or with orange and lemon rind, but the fruits, being quite highly flavored themselves, require little or no extra flavoring. Hot compotes make perfect desserts for the winter, not only because they are warming, but also because they are full of vitamins. Chilled compotes will keep well for up to a week in the refrigerator, and may also be used to make a refreshing start to the day by being served with breakfast.

Compotes can be made with a single fruit, but it is more interesting to have a mixture. So that the cooked fruits retain their shape as much as is possible they should be added to the sugar syrup in the order of cooking time – those that need the longest time first, and so on. Always select ripe, but firm fruits. A little liqueur may be added to a compote, just enough to enhance the flavor, not to overpower it.

Spring rhubarb needs careful cooking. It is very delicate and can easily break up.

basic sugar syrup	3 lb rhubarb, cut into
2 tablespoons (1½ oz)	2 inch pieces
fresh ginger root,	
peeled and finely	SERVES SIX
shredded	

Make the sugar syrup in a shallow, wide saucepan. Add the ginger and cook gently for 2–3 minutes.

Add just enough rhubarb to make a single layer. Cook gently for 5–6 minutes until just tender, turning the pieces frequently. Transfer to a serving dish. Continue until all the rhubarb is cooked. Boil the syrup until reduced and slightly thickened, then pour it over the rhubarb. Serve the compote hot or cold.

Basic sugar syrup
1⅓ cups sugar

Put the sugar into a saucepan with 1¼ cups of cold water. Heat very gently until the sugar has completely dissolved, then bring to a boil and boil the syrup for 1 minute.

Summer Compote

Serve this compote, well chilled, on bright, hot, sunny days with crème Chantilly. Or, cheer up a gloomy rainy day by serving it hot.

basic sugar syrup	1 lb ripe apricots,
1 lb ripe peaches or	skinned, halved and
nectarines, skinned,	pitted
halved, pitted and cut	1 lb dark cherries, pitted
into thick slices	
	SERVES SIX TO EIGHT

Make the sugar syrup in a large wide saucepan. Add the peach slices and cook gently for 10–15 minutes until barely tender. Add the apricots and cook for a further 5 minutes until the apricots just begin to soften. Add the cherries and cook just long enough to soften them without them losing their color, about 3 minutes.

Carefully transfer the fruits and their syrup to a serving bowl. Cool, then chill.

Fall Compote

Select very small pears for this compote. Lemon juice added to the syrup prevents the pears and apples discoloring, and adds a tangy flavor.

basic sugar syrup	1 lb plums, skinned and
strained juice of 1 lemon	pitted
1 lb small ripe, but firm	
pears	SERVES SIX TO EIGHT
1 lb Golden Delicious	
apples	

Make the sugar syrup in a large saucepan, adding the lemon juice. Thinly peel the pears, cut in half and remove the center core (if only large pears are available, cut the pears into quarters). Add the pears to the syrup and cook very gently for about 10–15 minutes until barely tender. While the pears are cooking, prepare the apples.

Core the apples with an apple corer, then peel the apples thinly. Cut the apples in half, then cut into slices across the halves, about ¼ inch thick. Add the apple slices to the pears and continue to cook for about 5 minutes until the apple slices are just tender.

Add the plums and cook for a further 5 minutes. Carefully transfer the fruits and juice to a serving bowl, taking care not to break up the fruits. Serve the compote hot or cold.

Winter Compote

A compote with a bittersweet flavor, tangy and refreshing.

basic sugar syrup	6 oz purple grapes
1 lb kumquats, thickly	6 oz green or white
sliced	grapes
1 lb clementines or	6 oz cranberries
tangerines, peeled and	
segmented	SERVES SIX TO EIGHT

Make the sugar syrup in a wide saucepan. Add the kumquats, cover and cook gently for about 15–20 minutes, until barely tender.

Add the clementines and grapes, then cook for a further 5 minutes, gently turning the fruits in the syrup and taking care not to break them up. Add the cranberries and cook for about 5 minutes until softened.

Carefully transfer the fruits and syrup to a serving bowl. Serve hot or cold.

Raspberry Sherbet

Loganberries or blackberries may be used instead of raspberries, to make equally delicious sherbets with a rich color and sharp flavor.

1⅓ cups sugar	strained juice of 1 large
¾ cup water	lemon
1 lb fresh raspberries	
	SERVES SIX TO EIGHT

Put the sugar into a saucepan with the water and heat gently until the sugar has dissolved, brushing the sides of the saucepan down with hot water. Bring to a boil and boil for 1 minute. Remove from the heat and allow to cool.

Press the raspberries through a nylon sieve or purée in a blender or food processor then sieve to remove the seeds.

Blend the raspberry purée, lemon juice and the sugar syrup together. Pour into a shallow container and freeze for about 3½ hours, until softly frozen, removing from the freezer every hour and beating well. Spoon into chilled glasses and serve.

Note
If using a food processor, allow the sherbet to freeze solid, then remove from the freezer and spoon half of it into the processor. Blend until very smooth and creamy, but still softly frozen, remove from the processor and repeat with the remaining half. Spoon the sherbet into chilled glasses and serve immediately. Or, return the sherbet to a container, cover, and freeze for later use. Remove the sherbet from the freezer for 15–20 minutes before serving.

The sherbet can be frozen in an ice cream maker.

Mango and Passion Fruit Sherbet

Although two complementing flavors are used for this sherbet, the distinctive flavor of each one still comes through.

1⅓ cups sugar	8 passion fruit
¾ cup water	strained juice of 1 lemon
5 ripe mangoes	
	SERVES SIX TO EIGHT

Put the sugar into a saucepan with the water and heat gently until the sugar has dissolved, brushing the sides of the saucepan down with hot water. Bring to a boil and boil for 1 minute. Remove from the heat and allow to cool.

Scoring through the mango skin, in quarters, pull the skin off, then cut the flesh away from the seed. Any ripe flesh that has been pulled away with the skin should be carefully cut away with a small sharp knife. Purée the flesh in a blender or food processor.

Cut the passion fruits in half, then scoop out the seeds with a small spoon into a nylon sieve placed over a small mixing bowl. Work the seeds in the sieve with a spoon to extract all the juice.

Blend the puréed mangoes, passion fruit juice, lemon juice and sugar syrup together, then pour the mixture into a shallow container. Freeze the mixture for about 3½–4 hours until softly frozen, removing from the freezer every hour and whisking well.

Spoon the sherbet into chilled glasses and serve.

see *NOTE* for Raspberry Sherbet (left).

Pineapple Sherbet

So that the sherbet can be served in the empty shell, slice the top off a pineapple, then carefully cut the flesh from the skin using a grapefruit knife, leaving the skin intact. Freeze the empty pineapple shell and the top, for a frosted appearance.

1⅓ cups sugar	strained juice of 2 large
¾ cup water	lemons
1 large pineapple, to give	strained juice of 1 large
1 lb 6 oz of prepared	orange
fruit, after the skin and	
core are removed	SERVES SIX TO EIGHT

Put the sugar into a saucepan with the water and heat gently until the sugar has dissolved, brushing the sides of the saucepan with hot water. Bring to a boil and boil for 1 minute. Remove from the heat and allow to cool.

Cut the pineapple flesh into small pieces, then purée in a blender or food processor. Press the purée through a nylon sieve to remove any stringy pieces from the pineapple.

Blend the purée with the lemon and orange juice, and the sugar syrup. Pour into a shallow container and freeze for about 3½ hours until softly frozen, removing from the freezer every hour and whisking well. Spoon the sorbet into well-chilled glasses, or alternatively pile it into the frozen pineapple case, place the pineapple lid on top of the sorbet and serve immediately.

Note
If using a food processor, allow the sherbet to freeze solid, then remove from the freezer and spoon half of it into the processor. Blend until very smooth and creamy, but still softly frozen, remove from the processor and repeat with the remaining half. Spoon the sherbet into chilled glasses and serve immediately. Or, return the sherbet to a container, cover, and freeze for later use. Remove the frozen sherbet from the freezer for 15–20 minutes before serving to allow it to soften a little.

The sherbet can also be frozen in an ice cream maker, if wished.

German Rumtopf

A Rumtopf is a ceramic pot made especially for preserving fresh summer fruits in rum. Rumtopfs came into being as a result of German seafarers trying to take exotic fruits from the West Indies to Germany about 200 years ago.

Each time they tried, the fruits spoiled during the long voyage. But one day, they found that some fruits at the bottom of a rum barrel, which had either fallen in by chance, or were put there for the purpose of getting the last drop of rum out of the barrel, were perfectly preserved and tasted as if freshly picked from the tree – they had a delicious rum flavor too! From then on, exotic fruits were transported, in barrels, covered in rum. It wasn't long before German housewives learned that they could preserve home-grown fruits in the same way.

Start to make a rumtopf when the first fruits of summer appear, usually strawberries, and continue through the summer months, until the rumtopf is full. A cast-iron will is needed to resist the temptation to taste for two to three months, but it really is worth waiting. The maturing time coincides perfectly with Christmas for a festival treat.

Most fruit can be put into a rumtopf but those with a high water content, such as melon and apple, should be avoided as they can cause fermentation. Also, avoid blackberries, rhubarb and gooseberries, as their sharpness can impart a bitter flavor. All fruits used must be ripe, sound, and very clean. When all of the fruits have been used up, use the juice in drinks.

To begin
2½ cups sugar
1 lb firm ripe
   strawberries, hulled

Thereafter
1⅓ cups sugar to every
   1 lb of fruit, such as:-
raspberries, hulled
loganberries, hulled
red currants, and black
   currants
peaches, skinned halved
   and pitted
nectarines, skinned,
   halved and pitted
apricots, skinned, halved
   and pitted
plums, skinned, halved
   and pitted

purple and green or white
   grapes
cherries, pitted
pineapple, skinned, core
   removed and cut into
   small pieces
mango, skinned, and cut
   into dice or slices
papaya, skinned, seeds
   removed and cut into
   small slices
kiwi fruits, skinned and
   sliced
pears, peeled, cored and
   sliced

1 bottle of rum, no less
   than 80 proof

Wash and thoroughly dry the rumtopf.

Put the strawberries into a large bowl, sprinkle with the sugar and mix lightly together. Cover and leave to stand for 1 hour. Put the strawberries, sugar and any juices into the rumtopf and cover with rum to a depth of ½ inch.

Cover the surface with plastic wrap, then place a saucer on top of the plastic wrap to keep the fruit submerged. Cover with more plastic wrap, and the rumtopf lid. Put the rumtopf in a cool, airy cupboard.

Continue to add fruits to the rumtopf, soaking them with the stated amount of sugar first, and adding rum with every addition. When full, cover and store in a cool place for 2–3 months.

SUMMER PUDDING (page 38)

Oranges Cooked in Caramel

Although they are an old favorite, oranges cooked in caramel are still a very popular dessert. Serve with crème Chantilly. If only small oranges are available, allow two per person.

1⅓ cups sugar
¼ cup cold water
1¼ cups boiling water
6 large oranges

2–3 tablespoons Grand Marnier
crème Chantilly (see page 94), to serve

SERVES SIX

Put the sugar into a saucepan with the cold water and heat gently until the sugar has dissolved, brushing down the sides of the saucepan with hot water. Bring to a boil, then boil until the syrup turns a golden caramel color.

Immediately plunge the base of the saucepan into cold water to prevent the caramel darkening further. Carefully pour the boiling water into the pan. Return the caramel to the heat, and heat gently until it has completely dissolved into the water.

Meanwhile, thinly pare the rind from two of the oranges, taking care not to remove the white pith. Cut the rind into very fine shreds and set aside. Using a very sharp knife, remove the skin and white pith from all the oranges.

Put the oranges and the shredded rinds into the caramel, cover and cook them very gently for 25–30 minutes until the oranges are tender, but do not allow to overcook – they must retain a good shape. Turn the oranges frequently during cooking.

Transfer the oranges and their syrup to a large serving dish. Add the Grand Marnier, and allow to cool. Cover and chill.

Summer Pudding

You don't have to wait until summer to enjoy summer pudding; it can be made very successfully with frozen fruits. Traditionally, it is made with bread, but pound cake slices can be used instead. Always make summer pudding the day before you wish to serve it.

6 oz red currants
¾ lb black currants
1⅔ cups sugar
thinly pared rind of
  1 large orange, in one
  continuous spiral if
  possible
½ lb raspberries, hulled

½ lb loganberries, hulled
12 thick slices of white
  bread, about 2 days
  old, crusts removed
crème Chantilly (see page
  94) to serve

SERVES EIGHT

Put the red and black currants into a large saucepan with the sugar and orange rind. Cover and cook gently until the juices flow and the sugar has dissolved. Add the raspberries and loganberries, and continue cooking for about 5 minutes until they are softened. Remove from the heat and allow to cool.

Cut a round from one of the slices of bread, large enough to fit in the bottom of a deep 2-quart round bowl. Place the round in the bottom of the bowl, then line the sides of the bowl with slightly overlapping slices of bread; reserve the rest for the center and the top.

Remove the orange rind from the fruit. Spoon half of the fruit and juice into the lined bowl, then place a layer of bread on top. Add the remaining fruit and juice, them cover completely with the remaining bread. Cover the bread with plastic wrap, then place a small, flat plate on the top. Stand the bowl on a plate, to catch any juices that overflow. Place some heavy weights on top of the plate, then chill the pudding overnight.

To serve, gently loosen the pudding from the sides of the bowl with a long narrow spatula, then unmold on to a flat plate. Serve with crème Chantilly.

Pears Cooked in Red Wine

Once cooked, the pears will keep very well in refrigerator for up to a week – improving in flavor as the wine penetrates deeper into them. Always make at least one day before serving.

bottle of red wine
1 cup sugar
strained juice of 1 large
   orange
strained juice of 1 large
   lemon
4 inch piece of cinnamon
   stick

6 allspice berries
6–8 large ripe, but firm,
   pears
lightly whipped cream, to
   serve

SERVES SIX TO EIGHT

Put the red wine into a large stainless steel saucepan with the sugar, orange and lemon juice, and the spices. Heat gently until the sugar has dissolved, then bring to a boil and boil for 1 minute.

Carefully peel the pears, leaving their stalks on. Put the pears into the spiced wine. Cover and cook gently until the pears are just tender when pierced with the tip of a knife. Turn the pears frequently during cooking.

Using a slotted spoon, transfer the pears to a serving bowl and set aside. Bring the wine to a boil, then boil gently until it is reduced by about half. Pour the reduced wine over the pears, allow to cool, then cover and chill. Serve with lightly whipped cream.

The Perfect Fresh Fruit Salad

Fruit salad can be made with a single fruit, or with a mixture of an indefinite number, according to availability, a combination of three or four fruits that particularly complement each other, or as a tropical mix. Use as many fruits as are available, so that the flavors can intermingle to make a highly perfumed salad, as in this recipe. Do not use bananas in a fruit salad; their very strong flavor will dominate and spoil the overall taste.

2½ cups sugar
thinly pared rind and
  strained juice of
  1 lemon
2½ cups water
2 large apples
3 large pears, peeled
1 small pineapple, skin
  and core removed, cut
  into small slices
1 small ripe melon, seeds
  removed, flesh
  removed with a melon
  baller
3 large oranges, skin and
  all white pith removed,
  then cut into segments
4 oz purple grapes,
  halved and seeds
  removed
4 oz green or white
  grapes, halved and
  seeds removed

½ lb dark sweet cherries,
  pitted
½ lb plums, skinned,
  pitted and sliced
1 large ripe mango,
  peeled and cut into thin
  slices
3 large peaches, skinned,
  pitted and sliced thinly
½ lb strawberries, hulled
  and sliced
½ lb raspberries, hulled
3 kiwi fruit, peeled and
  sliced
lightly whipped cream, to
  serve

SERVES TWELVE

Put the sugar and lemon rind in a large saucepan with the water. Heat gently until the sugar has dissolved, then bring to a boil and boil for 5 minutes. Stir in the lemon juice and allow to cool.

Remove the rind, then pour into a bowl.

Quarter, core and thinly slice the apples and pears. Add them to the syrup, then stir in the other fruits. Mix the salad gently, then cover with plastic wrap. Chill for 1 hour and serve with cream.

Melon and Figs in Brandy

This simple dessert with its contrasting textures and tastes, is perfect for a hot summer day.

⅔ cup sugar
2 tablespoons lemon juice
3 tablespoons brandy
half a large ripe
  honeydew melon

12 ripe figs
whipped cream, to serve
  (optional)

SERVES SIX

Put the sugar into a serving bowl with the lemon juice and brandy. Stir until sugar has dissolved.

Remove the seeds from the melon and scoop out the flesh with a melon baller, into the bowl.

Wipe the figs with paper towels. Taste a little piece from one of the figs. If the skin tastes bitter, peel the figs; if the skin does not taste bitter, do not peel. Cut the figs into quarters, then add them to the melon and mix lightly together.

Cover the bowl and leave to stand in a cool place, not the refrigerator, for 2 hours. Serve with cream.

FRESH FRUIT TARTLETS (page 48)

Strawberry and Loganberry Gelatin

The subtle taste of puréed strawberries and loganberries combine to make this flavorful gelatin. Other fruits can be used in the same way.

1⅓ cups sugar	**Decoration**
1¼ cups water, plus	1 cup heavy cream,
6 tablespoons	whipped
1 lb strawberries	fresh strawberries
1 lb loganberries or	
raspberries	SERVES EIGHT
2 tablespoons unflavored	
gelatin	

Put the sugar into a saucepan with the 1¼ cups water and heat gently until the sugar has dissolved. Bring to a boil, and boil for 1 minute. Remove from the heat and allow to cool.

Purée the fruits in a blender or food processor, then sieve to remove the seeds.

Sprinkle the gelatin over the remaining water in a small bowl. Stand in a pan of hot water and stir until dissolved.

Stir the hot gelatin into the sugar syrup, then stir into the fruit purée, until well blended. Pour the mixture into a 1½-quart mold and chill until set.

To unmold, dip the mold up to the rim in hot water for 5 seconds, then place a plate upside down over the mold. Invert the two, giving them a good shake. Lift off the mold.

Decorate the gelatin with whipped cream and fresh strawberries. Chill until ready to serve.

Blueberry Fool

When blueberries are not available, make this fool with black currants, red currants, gooseberries or rhubarb. Rhubarb and gooseberries may be cooked with brown sugar for added flavor. Shortbread fans make a perfect accompaniment.

½ lb blueberries or black	1¼ cups milk
currants	2 cups heavy cream
⅔ cup sugar	
6 egg yolks	SERVES SIX

Put the blueberries and ½ cup sugar into a saucepan, cover and cook gently until the berries soften. Press through a nylon sieve to purée. Chill.

Lightly whisk the egg yolks and the remaining sugar together. Heat the milk until it is almost boiling, then whisk into the egg yolks. Cook the custard over a pan of hot water water until it thickens enough to coat the back of a wooden spoon (or, cook the custard in a microwave oven on full power, for 2½–3 minutes, stirring every 30 seconds with a wire whisk). Immediately the custard thickens, pour it through a nylon sieve into a clean bowl. Cover the surface with plastic wrap to prevent a skin forming, cool, then refrigerate until very cold.

Whip the cream until it will hold soft peaks. Mix the chilled purée and custard together until well blended, then carefully fold in the whipped cream. Pour the fool into serving glasses and chill.

Fresh Fruit Purées

When puréed, fruit is transformed into one of its more versatile forms, and can be used as a topping, sauce, flavoring for soufflés, mousses and creams or to make fruit gelatin molds. Make soft fruits, and cooked fruits, into a purée by simply pressing them through a nylon sieve with the back of a wooden spoon or purée in a blender or food processor. Seeded fruits, such as strawberries, raspberries, and currants, should then be passed through a nylon sieve to remove their seeds. Strawberries have very small seeds, so use the finest mesh sieve you can – to completely remove their seeds, squeeze the purée through cheesecloth.
Firmer fruits, such as peaches, nectarines, apricots, red and black currants, need to be softened first by being cooked with a little water (just sufficient to prevent them sticking) and with a little sugar. Apples, rhubarb, gooseberries and plums must all be cooked with sugar, until soft, then puréed.

Flambéed Apples Triberg-Style

This wonderful way of cooking apples comes from Triberg, a small picturesque town in the Black Forest – famous for its Kirsch and its clocks! The apples are cooked with honey and lemon, then flambéed with Kirsch, and may be cooked on a spirit burner at the dining table.

6 large Golden Delicious, apples	strained juice of 1 lemon
3 tablespoons unsalted butter	3 tablespoons clear honey
3 tablespoons sugar	¼ cup Kirsch
thinly pared rind of 1 lemon, taken in one continuous spiral if possible	¾ cup heavy cream, lightly whipped with 1 tablespoon Kirsch, to serve
	SERVES FOUR TO SIX

Peel, quarter and core the apples. Cut each quarter into half again. Put the butter, sugar, lemon rind and juice and honey into a large shallow saucepan. Heat gently, stirring, until slightly thickened.

Add the apples to the mixture and cook gently, turning the pieces frequently, for 10–15 minutes until the apples are just tender when pierced with the tip of a knife. Spoon the juices into a serving pitcher and set aside.

Add the Kirsch to the apples, heat for 10 seconds, then set alight. Flambée the apples until the flames begin to subside, then spoon the apples, still slightly flaming, on to hot serving plates. Serve immediately with the juices and whipped cream.

Peaches with Loganberry Sauce

The following method for poaching peach halves can be used for other fruits, such as nectarines, pears, pineapple and plums. The syrup is not needed for the dessert, so store it in a covered container in the refrigerator for poaching other fruits at a later date – eliminating the need to make a fresh syrup. It may be used several times, but should not be used once it becomes discolored. Fruits should be poached until they are only just tender, as they will continue to cook a little more as they cool in the syrup.

4 very large ripe, but firm peaches	*Topping*
2 cups sugar	¾ cup heavy cream
2½ cups water	½ teaspoon vanilla extract
1 vanilla bean	1 tablespoon confectioners' sugar
	chopped pistachio nuts for sprinkling
Loganberry sauce	
½ lb loganberries	
½ lb sugar	SERVES FOUR
2 tablespoons Kirsch	

Put the peaches into a large bowl and cover with boiling water. Allow to stand for 1 minute, then remove the peaches and peel off their skins. Halve them and remove the pits.

Put the sugar into a large, wide saucepan with the water and vanilla bean. Heat gently until the sugar has dissolved, then bring to a boil and boil for 2 minutes. Add the peaches and cook very gently, so that the water barely simmers, until the peaches are just tender when pierced with the tip of a knife. Remove from the heat, allow to cool in the syrup. Discard the bean, then chill.

Put the loganberries into a bowl with the sugar and Kirsch, mix lightly, then cover and leave to stand for about 1 hour. Press through a nylon sieve to form a purée. Chill.

To serve, whip the cream with the vanilla and confectioners' sugar until it will hold soft peaks. Lift the peaches from the syrup with a slotted spoon and allow to drain well. Arrange the peach halves, in pairs, in serving glasses to form an open version of their original shape.

Spoon or pipe the cream into the center of the peaches, in neat whirls. Pour the loganberry sauce into the bottom of each glass without pouring over the peaches and cream. Sprinkle with nuts and serve immediately.

APRICOT TART (page 50)

Tarts and Pies

FROM a humble pie to the most exquisite tart filled with exotic fruits, tarts and pies are popular the world over. But, classifying just what is a tart, and what is a pie, can cause some confusion. Each one has a different image, depending on which country you live in and even within each country itself.

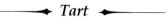

Tart

Technically speaking, a tart is an open pastry case filled with fruit, cream or a custard filling. They can be as simple as a round of pastry placed on a baking sheet and topped with fruit. Or, the pastry can be formed in a metal flan ring, or tart pan, to make an attractive container perfect for filling. The pastry used for tarts may be rich pie pastry, pâte sucrée, or almond pastry. The pastry case may be filled before baking, but more often that not, it is baked "blind" (without a filling) to be filled when it is cooked.

It may be baked blind with, or without, baking beans to weight the pastry down and keep it in shape. If the pastry is well formed, and chilled before baking it shouldn't be necessary to use baking beans, but to simply prick the pastry well over the bottom and up the sides with a fork. However, if using beans remove them for the last 5–10 minutes baking, for the pastry to dry completely. When a pastry case is to be filled with a custard mixture, it is advisable to partially bake it blind before adding the filling.

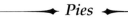

Pies

A pie is defined as having a bottom, sides and top, containing a filling. It can be made with a single pastry crust, to cover fruit in a deep pie pan or, be made with a double crust – pastry top and bottom – in a shallow pan.

Pies can be round, oval, oblong, or square. Sweet pies are usually made with either basic pie pastry, or rich pie pastry. Double crust pies may have a cleverly interwoven top, made with strips of pastry. A solid top may be left plain, or be decorated with pastry leaves, or other pretty shapes.

Pie edges always look better when decorated. The edge can be tapped lightly with a small knife to give a flaked effect, or it can be pressed down with the tines of a fork. It can be shaped into scallops by just pulling it in at close intervals with the tip of a knife.

A pie with a sweet filling should have the scallops made fairly small, and close together – as opposed to an entrée pie where the scallops are larger and wider apart (a tradition handed down from years gone by, when it was a means of identifying whether a pie had a sweet filling or a savory filling; probably in the old pie-making shops). A simple decorative edge can be made by pinching the edge between your forefinger and thumb, or with a pair of pastry crimpers.

The pastry may be glazed with beaten egg or milk before baking, or left unglazed and then sprinkled with sugar immediately the pie is removed from the oven. The top of a pie should be pricked in several places with a fork to allow the steam inside to escape.

Fillings

It would be an almost impossible task to list all of the fillings suitable for tarts and pies. The varieties are endless, but they do fall into three categories – fruit, cream and custards.

Double crust pies and lattice-topped pies can be filled with uncooked or pre-cooked fruits. Uncooked fruit benefits from being tossed in a little flour, as the flour will thicken the juice from the fruit as the pie cooks. Ground almonds sprinkled over the bottom layer of pastry for a fruit pie will help to prevent the pastry from becoming soggy.

Tart cases are particularly good for filling with fresh fruits, any type of cream or mousse mixture. Flavored and spiced custard mixtures can be baked in a pastry case until set.

The French are particularly famous for their tarts, especially those filled with fresh fruits. Their most famous tart must be the apple tart from Normandy (see page 50) as well as many others that contain a sweetened custard and fruit.

Americans have long prided themselves on their apple pies. We boast of having the best flavored apples, so our pies should be good! In Britain, the Elizabethans added wine to their apple pies, and there's no reason why we shouldn't too. The next time you cook apples prior to putting them into a pie, add a little red or white wine. It has also long been the custom to add spices and flavorings, such as lemon and orange rind.

Fresh Fruit Tartlets

These colorful little tartlets can be made with any fresh fruits you like. Raspberries can be sifted with confectioners' sugar instead of being glazed.

1 quantity of almond pastry (see page 92)
half quantity of crème pâtissière (see page 93)
4 oz dark, well-flavored, cherries, pitted and halved
4 oz purple grapes, halved and seeded
4 oz green or white grapes, halved and seeded
2 kiwi fruit, peeled and sliced

finely chopped nuts or toasted sliced almonds, for sprinkling (optional)

Apricot glaze
⅔ cup apricot jam
1 tablespoon Kirsch

Red currant glaze
⅓ cup red currant jelly

MAKES TWELVE

Roll out the pastry on a lightly floured surface and cut out twelve 5-inch circles with a round cutter and use to line twelve 4-inch tartlet pans. Trim the edges and prick the bottom of each tartlet with a fork, then place the lined pans on baking sheets and chill for at least 30 minutes.

Bake blind in a preheated 425° oven for 20–25 minutes until very lightly browned. Allow the cases to cool a little in their pans, then carefully transfer to a wire rack to cool.

Make the apricot glaze (see page 94), then brush it evenly over the inside of each pastry case. Reserve the remaining glaze.

Divide the crème pâtissière equally between the pastry cases and spread it evenly. Arrange the cherries attractively in three of the cases, the grapes in six, and the kiwi fruit in the remaining ones.

Reheat the remaining apricot glaze until boiling, then carefully brush it over the green grapes and the kiwi fruit to glaze them evenly. Heat the red currant jelly until boiling, then carefully brush it over the cherries and the black grapes.

Once glazed, the fruits may be sprinkled with finely chopped nuts or a few toasted sliced almonds, if liked. Serve as soon as possible.

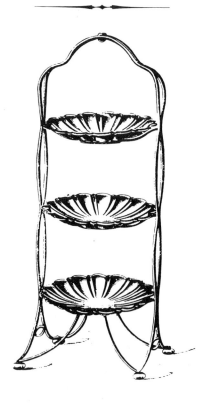

FRENCH APPLE TART (page 50)

Apricot Tart

It is best to use fresh apricots for this tart, but when they are not available you can use canned or bottled ones.

about 17 fresh apricots, poached or use 34 canned or bottled apricot halves	2 teaspoons sugar
	1 tablespoon apricot jam
2 tablespoons Kirsch	*Decoration*
1 quantity of pâte sucrée (see page 92)	¾ cup heavy cream
	1 oz semi-sweet chocolate, melted
½ cup light cream	
1 egg	SERVES SIX TO EIGHT

Put the apricot halves into a bowl, sprinkle with the Kirsch, cover and let stand for about 1 hour.

Roll out the pâte sucrée on a lightly floured surface to a round, 1 inch larger than a 9-inch fluted tart pan. Line the pan with the pastry, pressing it well into the flutes. Trim the edge, and prick the pastry all over with a fork. Chill for 30 minutes, then partially bake in a preheated 425° oven for 20 minutes.

Meanwhile, drain the apricots, reserving any Kirsch. Lightly whisk the cream with the egg, sugar and remaining Kirsch.

Remove the partially baked tart case from the oven. Reduce the oven temperature to 375°. Leaving the pastry case in the pan, spread the apricot jam over the bottom of the tart case. Reserve six apricot halves for decoration, then arrange the rest on top of the jam. Pour in the custard mixture. Bake for 30–40 minutes until the custard is set. Cool.

Whip the cream for the decoration until it will hold soft peaks. Transfer the tart to a serving plate and spread the cream evenly over the top. Put the melted chocolate into a small paper pastry bag, then cut a small hole in the bottom of the bag. Pipe the chocolate, in criss-cross lines, across the cream. Cut each of the reserved apricot halves in half and arrange neatly around the edge of the tart on the cream to decorate.

French Apple Tart

Because it is attributed to the apple growing region of France, this tart is sometimes called Normandy Apple Tart. This recipe, which is just one of many versions, uses two types of apples, cooked in different ways, each one contrasting with the other. If you do not have Calvados or applejack, use brandy.

2 lb tart apples	4–5 large Golden Delicious apples
1⅓ cups sugar	
2 tablespoons water	half quantity apricot glaze (see page 94)
⅓ cup (2 oz) raisins	
¼ cup Calvados or applejack	crème Chantilly (see page 94), to serve
1 quantity pâte sucrée (see page 92)	SERVES EIGHT

Peel, quarter, core and slice the tart apples and put into a large saucepan with 1 cup of the sugar and the water. Cover and cook gently for about 20 minutes until the apples become soft and fluffy. Pour the cooked apples into a nylon sieve placed over a bowl;

allow to drain and cool. (The apple juice will not be needed.)

Put the raisins into a small saucepan with the Calvados and cook gently for 2–3 minutes to soften the raisins. Allow to cool.

Roll out the pâte sucrée on a lightly floured surface to a round, 1 inch larger than a 10-inch fluted tart pan. Line the pan with the pastry, pressing it well into the flutes. Trim the edges.

Beat the cooked apples until fairly smooth, then fold in the raisins and Calvados. Spread the apple mixture evenly over the bottom of the pastry case. Peel and core the Golden Delicious apples. Cut each apple in half, then cut each half into thin slices.

Arrange the apple slices in concentric circles on top of the cooked apple mixture. Sprinkle the apple slices with the remaining sugar. Bake in a preheated 425° oven for 30–35 minutes until the pastry is cooked, and the apple slices are tender and very lightly browned.

Heat the apricot glaze until boiling. Immediately the tart is removed from the oven, brush the apricot glaze evenly over the apple slices. Allow the tart to cool to room temperature before serving. Serve with lightly whipped crème Chantilly.

Strawberry Tart

This classic, French strawberry tart is simplicity itself, but you must use full-flavored strawberries and a good strawberry jam to produce the best results.

1 quantity of almond pastry (see page 92)
1½ cups strawberry jam
3 tablespoons Cointreau
1½ lb medium-sized, fresh strawberries, hulled

lightly whipped cream, to serve

SERVES EIGHT

Roll out the almond pastry on a lightly floured surface to a round, 1 inch larger than a 10-inch fluted tart pan. Line the pan with the pastry, pressing it well into the flutes. Trim the edges, then prick the pastry all over. Chill for at least 30 minutes, then bake in a preheated 425° oven for 25–30 minutes until very lightly browned. Allow to cool.

Put the strawberry jam into a saucepan, heat gently until melted, then sieve through a nylon sieve into another clean saucepan. Stir in the Cointreau and bring to a boil.

Brush a little of the strawberry glaze over the bottom and up the sides of the pastry case. Put the pastry case on a flat serving plate. Arrange the strawberries, pointed ends up, neatly in the pastry case. Spoon the remaining strawberry glaze over the strawberries until they are all evenly coated. Serve with lightly whipped cream.

Whiskey Mocha Tart

This tart is made with a coffee-flavored bavarois mixture, topped with whiskey cream, and elegantly decorated with chocolate caraque.

---

half quantity of rich pie
   pastry (see page 88)
5 oz semi-sweet chocolate
2 teaspoons unflavored
   gelatin
2 tablespoons water
¾ cup milk
1 tablespoon instant
   coffee
3 egg yolks

1 tablespoon sugar
¾ cup heavy cream

Topping
1 cup heavy cream
1–2 tablespoons whiskey
1 tablespoon sugar

SERVES SIX TO EIGHT

Roll out the pastry on a lightly floured surface to a round 1 inch larger than a 9 inch fluted tart pan. Line the pan with the pastry, pressing it well into the flutes. Trim the edges then prick the pastry with a fork. Chill for 30 minutes, then bake blind in a preheated 425° oven for 20–25 minutes until the pastry is cooked and very lightly browned. Allow to cool.

Break the chocolate into small pieces and put into a small bowl over a pan of hot water until the chocolate melts. Stir until smooth.

Remove the pastry case from the tart pan and place it, upside-down, on a sheet of wax paper. Using a pastry brush, brush some of the melted chocolate evenly all over the pastry case. Leave in a cool place until the chocolate sets. Turn the tart case over and brush the inside with more chocolate and allow to set.

Spread out the remaining chocolate thinly on a marble slab, or on wax paper and leave to set until it no longer sticks to your hand when you touch it. Holding a large knife with both hands, push the blade across the surface of the chocolate to roll pieces off in long curls. Adjust the angle of the blade to get the best curls. Put the curls on a plate and chill until needed.

Sprinkle the gelatin over the water in a small bowl and set aside.

Put the milk and the coffee granules into a small saucepan, heat gently until the coffee dissolves completely, and the milk comes almost to a boil. Very lightly whisk the egg yolks and the sugar together in a bowl, then stir in the coffee-flavored milk until well combined.

Place the bowl over a pan of hot water and cook the custard, stirring continuously, until thick enough to coat the back of the spoon, (alternatively, cook the custard in a microwave oven on full power for 2–2½ minutes, stirring every 30 seconds).

Immediately the custard thickens, strain it through a nylon sieve into a clean bowl. Add the soaked gelatin and stir until dissolved. Allow the custard to cool, stirring frequently to prevent a skin forming.

Whip the cream until it will just hold soft peaks, then gently fold it into the coffee custard. Place the chocolate coated tart case on a flat serving plate, fill with the coffee cream mixture, then chill until set.

Make the topping: whip the cream with the whiskey and sugar until it will just hold soft peaks, then spread an even layer of cream over the top of the tart. Whip the remaining cream until thick enough to pipe and fill a pastry bag fitted with a medium sized star tip. Pipe whirls of cream around the top of the tart, then decorate with the chocolate flakes. Chill until ready to serve.

WHISKEY MOCHA TART (above)

Tray-Baked Tarts

These tarts are reminiscent of those made in a favorite café of mine in Switzerland. In the fall, they make huge trays of plum tarts and serve portions topped with a mound of whipped cream nearly as big as the Jungfrau mountain that one sits and admires from the café terrace.

Once you have made one tart, you will soon realize that you do not really need a recipe to follow. You simply roll out rich pie pastry as large, or as small, as you wish, to fit your baking sheet. The pastry is then covered with apples, plums, halved pears or apricots, sprinkled with sugar and baked – easy to make, and so delicious to eat! Use marmalade for apple tart or apricot glaze (see page 94) for the other fruit.

1 quantity of rich pie pastry (see page 88)	⅔ cup sugar
1½–2 lb apples	¼ cup fine shred orange marmalade
⅓ cup (2 oz) ground almonds	lightly whipped cream, to serve

SERVES EIGHT TO TEN

Roll out the pastry on a lightly floured surface to an oblong about 12×13 inches, or if your baking sheet is very flat – roll the pastry out on the baking sheet directly. Place the pastry on the baking sheet, then turn in the edge about ½ inch to form a small edge. Pinch the pastry edge, with your forefinger and thumb, to decorate.

Core and peel the apples and slice into rings about ¼ inch thick. Sprinkle the ground almonds over the pastry, then arrange the apple rings, overlapping, in neat rows on top. Sprinkle with sugar, then bake in a preheated 425° oven for 30–35 minutes until the pastry is cooked and lightly browned, and the apples are tender.

Heat the marmalade until boiling, then brush it evenly over the hot apples to glaze. Serve the tart cut into slices, with lightly whipped cream.

Angostura Pie

Normally associated with cocktails and hangovers, Angostura bitters is surprisingly good when it is sweetened and mixed with cream – as it is in this creamy pie.

1 quantity of pâte sucrée (see page 92)	*Decoration* ¾ cup crème Chantilly (see page 94)
2 eggs, separated	14–16 pistachio nuts, skinned
⅓ cup sugar	
1 tablespoon unflavored gelatin	
3 tablespoons water	SERVES SIX TO EIGHT
1½ tablespoons Angostura bitters	
1¼ cups heavy cream	

Roll out the pâte sucrée on a lightly floured surface and use to line an 8-inch pie or quiche pan. Trim and decorate the edge. Prick the pastry all over with a fork. Chill for 30 minutes, then bake blind in a preheated 425° oven for 20–25 minutes until the pastry is cooked. Allow to cool.

Beat the egg yolks with the sugar until very thick, then beat in the Angostura bitters.

Sprinkle the gelatin over the water in a small bowl. Stand the bowl of gelatin in a small saucepan of hot water and stir until dissolved. Whip the cream until it will hold soft peaks. Beat the egg whites until they are quite foamy, but not too stiff.

Whisk the gelatin into the Angostura mixture, then carefully fold in the cream and the egg whites. Pour the mixture, immediately, into the pie case. Chill until set.

Whip the crème Chantilly until thick enough to pipe, then fill a pastry bag fitted with a large star tip. Pipe rosettes, or stars, of cream on top of the pie, then decorate with pistachio nuts. Chill the pie until ready to serve.

Old-Fashioned Apple Pie

This is the sort of pie our grandmothers used to make – simple and straightforward, but full of flavor. Serve the pie warm, with a real egg custard sauce. Blackberry, blackberry and apple, and rhubarb pies can be made in exactly the same way.

about 2 lb tart apples	8–12 cloves
¾ cup sugar	1 quantity of basic pie
3 tablespoons flour	pastry (see page 88)
finely grated rind of	sugar for sprinkling
1 lemon	
2 tablespoons lemon juice	SERVES FOUR

Peel, quarter and slice the apples and put into a large bowl with the sugar, flour, lemon rind, lemon juice and cloves. Toss gently together.

Roll out the pastry on a lightly floured surface to an oval, about 2 inches larger than the top of a 1-quart oval baking dish or deep pie dish. Cut a 1-inch strip from the outer edge and place it on the dampened rim of the dish.

Fill the pie dish with the apple mixture, forming it into a neat mound. Brush the pastry strip with water, then carefully cover the pie dish with the remaining pastry, pressing the pastry edges together well to seal. Trim the pastry from around the edge of the pie with a small sharp knife, holding the knife at an angle pointed away from the pie.

Pressing firmly around the edge of the pastry, gently tap the pastry with a small knife to flake the edge, then decorate the edge by pulling it into small scallops with the tip of the knife. Make a small hole in the center of the pie to allow the steam to escape. Chill for about 30 minutes.

Bake in a preheated 425° oven for 10 minutes, then reduce the oven temperature to 400° and continue cooking for 30–35 minutes until the pastry is golden brown, and the apples are cooked.

Immediately the pie is removed from the oven, sift sugar evenly over the top.

Hot Soufflés

S WITH time, a hot soufflé waits for no man – even the most exalted in the land must wait for a soufflé.

To some, a hot soufflé means a dramatic end to a dinner, as is certainly the case when a golden, puffed-up masterpiece is triumphantly carried to the dining table. Others prefer to serve a hot soufflé at a cosy, more intimate dinner for two or four, especially during the winter, when it makes the perfect dessert – warming, yet very light. Making a soufflé in a more relaxed atmosphere means that there is less risk of embarrassment if it fails to rise to one's expectations. When the cook is not under any stress they always rise well!

A hot soufflé is the true soufflé. In a cold soufflé the tiny bubbles of air, trapped within the egg whites, are set in suspension by the gelatin. With a hot soufflé, the tiny air bubbles expand as they are heated, puffing up the base mixture, to which they were added, by as much as two-thirds of its original size.

The base for a sweet soufflé is usually a flavored sauce, enriched with egg yolks, anything from a subtle vanilla, through a whole range of fruit purées, to the stronger flavors of coffee and chocolate. The sauce must be just the right consistency for incorporating egg whites – neither thick, nor thin. Having said that, soufflés can be more simply made with fruit purée and meringue, though using a slightly different technique (see the next page).

The success of a soufflé depends on the egg whites being beaten to the right degree, and how they are added to the base mixture. They should be beaten until they are stiff enough to hold a stiff, unwavering, peak on the end of a beater, yet still be very smooth. Egg whites beaten by hand in a copper bowl produce a greater volume. A proportion of the sugar is beaten into the whites, to make them into a lighter, smoother meringue.

A little of the beaten whites should always be added to the sauce base to loosen the mixture, and make it easier to fold in the remaining whites. If the saucepan is large enough, the whites can all be added to the sauce in the pan. Always fold the egg whites into the base mixture very carefully, and very lightly. The more bubbles you retain within the mixture, the lighter the soufflé will be, and the more it will rise. Fold the whites in with a large metal spoon, or a rubber spatular.

Hot soufflés are normally baked in straight-sided ovenproof dishes. A soufflé dish should be buttered well and then be lightly coated with sugar. Only use butter; other fats would spoil the flavor of the soufflé. Buttering the dish enables the soufflé mixture to rise up the side of the dish without sticking, so that it can go on rising above the top of the dish until it reaches its maximum height and sets properly.

It is not necessary to put a paper collar around a dish for a hot soufflé; providing the mixture is of the right consistency it will support itself. Removing a paper collar puts the soufflé in danger of collapsing more quickly, and of being damaged by pulling a chunk out of the side with the paper. Stand the soufflé dish on a baking sheet, to help to transmit the heat more quickly through the dish, and to make it easier to remove from the oven when it is ready.

A soufflé can be baked until it is just set and still slightly moist in the center, or until completely set. Do not over bake a soufflé, it will become very dry. Cooking in a moderate oven means that the soufflé cooks evenly throughout. In a hot oven, it would rise quickly, form a crisp outside and have a soft center. To test for doneness, insert a long thin skewer into the center of the soufflé – if it comes out moist, the soufflé will be slightly soft; if it comes out clean, the soufflé will be set right through to the center.

Soufflés are usually dusted with confectioners' sugar as soon as they are taken out of the oven, so always have the sugar and a small sifter nearby. Serve the soufflé on a doily-lined plate; this makes it look more attractive, and also easier to carry to the table. Serving the soufflé with a complementing sauce makes it even more delicious.

Other soufflés

A soufflé made simply with meringue and a fruit purée is mixed in a slightly different way to other soufflés. As it is quite difficult to fold whites into a thin mixture, the purée is gradually mixed into the whites. As the whites are made into a strong meringue, they can withstand the extra mixing.

Steamed soufflés, instead of being baked in the oven, are gently steamed in a fairly deep saucepan in a bain-marie on top of the stove. The slow moist cooking sets the soufflé firm enough to be turned out, yet still wonderfully light, and with certainly no fear of it collapsing before it reaches the table.

With a soufflé omelette the yolks are beaten with sugar and flavoring until very thick then mixed with a little flour. The whites are beaten in the normal way before being added to the yolks. The mixture is cooked briefly in an omelette pan on top of the stove before being baked in the oven.

Soufflé mixtures can also be used as a filling for small crêpes, or be baked in scooped out orange cases.

Steamed Chocolate Soufflé with Chocolate Sauce

Those who have a passion for chocolate will find that this soufflé, with its rich chocolate sauce, will transport them to "seventh heaven!"

2 tablespoons unsalted butter
2½ tablespoons all purpose flour
⅔ cup milk
3 oz semi-sweet chocolate, chopped finely
2 tablespoons sugar
6 tablespoons heavy cream
3 egg yolks
4 egg whites
confectioners' sugar for sifting

Chocolate sauce
3 oz semi-sweet chocolate, chopped finely

2 tablespoons brandy
⅔ cup milk
⅔ cup heavy cream
1 tablespoon unsalted butter
2 teaspoons cornstarch, plus 1 tablespoon milk for mixing

SERVES SIX

Grease a 6 inch diameter, 3 inch deep, soufflé dish with butter, then coat evenly with a little sugar.

Melt the butter in a saucepan, then stir in the flour. Gradually stir in the milk, then add the chocolate. Heat gently, stirring all the time, until the chocolate melts, then bring to a boil and boil until thickened. Remove the sauce from the heat, beat in half the sugar, then the cream and the egg yolks.

Beat the egg whites until stiff, but not dry, then gradually beat in the remaining sugar, beating until shiny. Add about one-third of the egg whites to the chocolate mixture and fold in carefully to loosen the mixture, then very gently fold in the remaining egg whites.

Pour the soufflé mixture into the prepared dish. Place a trivet in a heavy-based saucepan, stand the soufflé dish on the trivet, then add enough boiling water to come about one-third of the way up the side of the dish. Cover the pan with a tightly fitting lid, then steam the soufflé gently for 45 minutes, until it is well risen and set.

Meanwhile, make the chocolate sauce: put the chocolate, brandy, milk and cream into a small saucepan. Heat gently, stirring until the chocolate melts, then stir in the butter.

Blend the cornstarch with the milk to form a smooth paste, then stir it into the sauce. Cook over a moderate heat until the sauce thickens slightly. Keep the sauce warm until ready to serve – to prevent a skin forming, cover the surface of the sauce closely with plastic wrap.

When the soufflé is cooked, turn the heat off under the pan and allow the soufflé to settle for 5 minutes. Turn the soufflé out onto a warmed serving dish and sift confectioners' sugar lightly on top. Serve immediately, with the chocolate sauce poured around it, or served separately in a pitcher.

Apricot Soufflé with Apricot Sauce

Canned or bottled apricot halves can be used for this recipe. Purée the apricots with their juice in a blender or food processor to get the best results.

2 tablespoons unsalted
  butter
2½ tablespoons all-
  purpose flour
14 oz canned apricots,
  puréed
⅓ cup sugar
3 egg yolks
4 egg whites
confectioners' sugar for
  sifting

Apricot sauce
14 oz canned apricots,
  puréed
1 tablespoon Grand
  Marnier
1 tablespoon sugar
1 teaspoon arrowroot

SERVES FOUR TO SIX

Grease a 6 inch diameter, 3 inch deep, soufflé dish with butter, then coat evenly with a little sugar.

Melt the butter in a saucepan, add the flour, then gradually stir in the apricot purée. Bring the sauce to a boil, stirring, and boil until the mixture thickens. Remove the sauce from the heat and beat in half the sugar, then the egg yolks.

Beat the egg whites until stiff, but not dry, then gradually beat in the remaining sugar, beating until shiny. Gradually fold the egg whites into the apricot sauce until no trace of white remains.

Pour the soufflé mixture into the prepared dish. Stand the dish on a baking sheet, then bake in the center of a preheated 350° oven for about 40 minutes, until very well risen, and just lightly set.

Meanwhile, make the apricot sauce: put the apricot purée, Grand Marnier, and sugar into a small saucepan. Blend the arrowroot with a little cold water to make a smooth paste, then stir into the apricot mixture. Bring the sauce to a boil, stirring until the mixture thickens and clears. Pour the sauce into a warmed serving pitcher and keep hot.

When the soufflé is cooked, remove from the oven and sift confectioners' sugar lightly over the top. Serve immediately with the apricot sauce.

Vanilla Soufflé

Serve this very light vanilla soufflé with lightly whipped créme Chantilly, a fruit sauce, or a vanilla-flavored custard sauce.

2 tablespoons unsalted
  butter
2½ tablespoons all-
  purpose flour
⅔ cup milk
⅓ cup sugar
2 tablespoons heavy
  cream
1 teaspoon vanilla extract

3 egg yolks
4 egg whites
confectioners' sugar for
  sifting

SERVES FOUR

Grease a 6 inch diameter, 3 inch deep, soufflé dish with butter, then coat evenly with a little sugar.

Melt the butter in a saucepan, add the flour, then gradually stir in the milk. Bring the sauce to a boil, stirring until the mixture thickens. Remove from the heat and beat in half the sugar, the heavy cream, vanilla and then the egg yolks.

Beat the egg whites until they are stiff, but not dry, then gradually beat in the remaining sugar, beating until shiny. Fold the egg whites into the vanilla sauce.

Pour the soufflé mixture into the prepared dish, then stand the dish on a baking sheet. Bake in the center of a preheated 350° oven for 45–50 minutes until the soufflé is very well risen, and lightly set. Remove from the oven and sift confectioners' sugar lightly over the top. Serve immediately.

Orange and Grand Marnier Soufflé

Serve this classic soufflé with very lightly whipped cream flavored with Grand Marnier.

grated rind of 2 large oranges	3 egg yolks
⅔ cup milk	4 egg whites
2 tablespoons unsalted butter	confectioners' sugar for sifting
2½ tablespoons all-purpose flour	
⅓ cup sugar	SERVES 4
2 tablespoons Grand Marnier	

Put the grated rind into a saucepan with the milk, bring almost to a boil, then remove from the heat, cover and let stand for 30 minutes, or longer if possible.

Grease a 6 inch diameter, 3 inch deep, soufflé dish with butter, then coat evenly with a little sugar.

Strain the milk through a small nylon sieve to remove the rind. Melt the butter in a saucepan, add the flour, then gradually stir in the orange-flavored milk. Bring to a boil, stirring until the mixture thickens. Remove the sauce from the heat and beat in half the sugar, the Grand Marnier, and then the egg yolks.

Beat the egg whites until they are stiff, but not dry, then gradually beat in the remaining sugar, beating until shiny. Fold the egg whites into the orange sauce.

Pour the soufflé mixture into the prepared dish, then stand the dish on a baking sheet. Bake in the center of a preheated 350° oven for 35–40 minutes until the soufflé is very well risen and lightly set. Remove from the oven and sift confectioners' sugar lightly over the top. Serve immediately.

OLD ENGLISH SYLLABUB (page 71)

Soufflé Crêpes with Blackberry Sauce

These little crêpes, filled with a tangy lemon mixture and baked, served with a blackberry sauce, are quite delicious. A supply of crêpes and blackberry sauce in the freezer, will make this a speedy dessert to prepare.

6 tablespoons all-purpose
   flour
a pinch of salt
1 egg
⅔ cup milk
1 tablespoon unsalted
   butter, melted
1 tablespoon brandy
butter for frying

Blackberry sauce
½ lb fresh or frozen
   blackberries
⅓–½ cup sugar

Soufflé filling
2 egg yolks
⅓ cup sugar
finely grated rind of
   1 lemon
1 tablespoon strained
   lemon juice
2 tablespoons all-purpose
   flour, sifted
3 egg whites
confectioners' sugar for
   sifting

SERVES FOUR TO EIGHT

Sift the flour and salt into a mixing bowl and make a well in the center. Break the egg into the center, then gradually beat into the flour, adding the milk as the mixture thickens. When the batter is smooth mix in the melted butter and brandy. Cover and let stand for about 30 minutes.

Heat a little butter in a 6-inch heavy-based frying pan, then pour off any excess. Pour in just enough batter to cover the bottom of the pan thinly. Cook for about 1 minute until the batter is set, and the crêpe is lightly browned on the underside, turn or toss the crêpe and cook the other side for about 1 minute until lightly browned. Transfer the crêpe to a plate and cover with a paper towel. Make seven more crêpes in the same way, placing paper between each one.

To make the sauce, sieve the blackberries through a nylon sieve into a small saucepan, then stir in the sugar to taste. Set aside until needed.

To make the soufflé filling, and complete the crêpes, butter a 9×11-inch ovenproof dish. Beat the egg yolks with half the sugar and the lemon rind until very thick, then beat in the lemon juice. Fold in the flour. Beat the egg whites until stiff, then gradually beat in the remaining sugar, beating until shiny. Fold the egg whites into the lemon mixture.

Spread the crêpes out on a work surface and divide the soufflé mixture equally between them, spooning it along the center of each one. Bring the sides of each crêpe up over the filling, until they just overlap. Place the crêpes side-by-side in the buttered dish, sift lightly with confectioners' sugar, then bake in the center of a preheated 375° oven for 12–15 minutes until the soufflé mixture is well risen and lightly firm to the touch.

Meanwhile, heat the blackberry sauce and pour it into a warmed serving pitcher. Remove the cooked crêpes from the oven and sift lightly with more confectioners' sugar. Serve immediately, with the hot blackberry sauce.

Raspberry Soufflé

Made simply with puréed raspberries, sugar and egg whites, this soufflé has a lovely fresh fruit flavor. Serve with a little lightly whipped cream, if liked.

½ lb fresh raspberries	confectioners' sugar for
3 egg whites	sifting
½ cup sugar	
	SERVES FOUR

Grease a 6 inch diameter, 3 inch deep, soufflé dish with butter, then coat evenly with a little sugar. Sieve the raspberries through a nylon sieve to make a purée, about 1 cup.

Beat the egg whites until stiff, but not dry, then gradually beat in the sugar, beating until shiny. Fold the raspberry purée into the egg whites.

Pour the soufflé mixture into the prepared soufflé dish and mark into a swirl on the top. Stand the dish on a baking sheet, then bake in a preheated 350° oven for about 20 minutes, until lightly set. Remove from the oven and sift confectioners' sugar lightly over the top. Serve immediately.

Salzburger Nockerln

This is a specialty of the Salzkammergut region of Austria. The soufflé is baked in a shallow dish, about 1 inch deep, and is mounded in the dish to represent the mountains of the area.

---

3 egg yolks	4 egg whites
finely grated rind of 2 lemons	⅓ cup sugar
	confectioners' sugar for sifting
2 tablespoons strained lemon juice	
2½ tablespoons all-purpose flour, sifted	SERVES 4

Butter a shallow 9 inch round, or oval, dish.

Beat the egg yolks and lemon rind together until they are thickened, then beat in the lemon juice and beat in the flour.

Beat the egg whites until they are stiff, but not dry, then gradually beat in the sugar, beating until shiny. Fold a little of the egg whites into the lemon mixture to loosen it, then carefully fold in the rest.

Spoon the soufflé mixture, in three mounds, in the prepared dish. Place the dish on a baking sheet and bake in the center of a preheated 375° oven for 12–14 minutes until lightly set. Remove from the oven and sift confectioners' sugar lightly over the top. Serve immediately.

Creams, Mousses and Cold Soufflés

AWE-INSPIRING soufflés, beautifully molded bavarois, and rich, light mousses are wonderful creations, guaranteed to bring sighs of ecstasy from dinner guests!

Eggs are the foundation for these recipes, with the yolks and the whites going their separate ways, to thicken, and to add volume and lightness. When heated, yolks will thicken cream or milk, to make a custard. Beaten whites add lightness and volume to soufflés and mousses. Yolks beaten with sugar become very thick, making them the perfect base for flavorings such as fruit juices and melted chocolate.

Cream adds richness, and when it is whipped it will add volume and lightness, too. Custards can be made with heavy or light cream, or with milk if you prefer a less rich mixture. Custard made with cream has a smooth velvety texture, which is why it can be served as a dessert in its own right, in the form of crème brûlée, or petits pots de crème. Bavarois is a classic dessert made with a rich custard, lightened with whipped cream, and set with gelatin. Bavarois, and other creamy mixtures can be set in decorative molds. Bavarois mixture can also be used as the filling for an elaborate cake, or sweet pastry tart case.

Cold soufflés are very light mixtures set high above a soufflé dish, as imitations of hot soufflés.

Making a custard

A custard is easily ruined if the mixture is overheated, and for this reason they are not usually cooked over direct heat, but in a double boiler or bowl placed over a saucepan of gently simmering hot water. Constant stirring is needed to prevent the mixture overheating in the bottom of the bowl. A slow, even cooking makes a smoother custard. Once thickened, the custard should be strained immediately, through a nylon sieve into a clean bowl. This cools the custard and removes any lumps.

Whipping cream

To enable cream to be blended smoothly with the mixture it is being added to, it should be of a similar consistency. Most of the desserts in this chapter require the cream to be whipped to a soft peak, or until it will only just hold the trail of the beater.

Use very fresh cream for whipping; the fresher it is, the longer it will take to whip. If the cream is not fresh, it will thicken with a few turns of the beater, becoming solid rather than light and airy. It should always be well chilled, and preferably whipped in a chilled mixing bowl.

If cream is overwhipped before it is blended with another mixture, it will continue to thicken as it is mixed in, making it very difficult to obtain a smooth mixture. Acid in fruit purée will thicken cream on contact, so it is better to slightly under whip it when the cream is to be added to a mixture containing a high percentage of acid purée.

☞

FROZEN PASSION FRUIT SOUFFLÉ (page 67)

The same happens when cream is added to fruit juice and wine, as when making a syllabub.

Gelatin

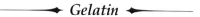

For molded creams to be turned out, and mousses and soufflés to retain their shape, they must be set with gelatin.

If gelatin is to be added to a cold mixture, it must be softened in a little cold liquid before being stirred over heat until completely dissolved. Alternatively, dissolve the gelatin directly in a larger quantity of very hot liquid, such as the custard for a bavarois. Be sure to stir until the gelatin is completely melted into the mixture.

Adding gelatin to a cold mixture is a little tricky because it must be completely dissolved first.

If cool gelatin is added to a cold mixture, it will set on contact with the mixture setting in fine threads, known as "roping." The mixture will not set properly or it will set the mixture too quickly, before you have a chance to fold in the egg whites or cream; either way, it will taste most unpleasant. Whisking the still hot gelatin into a mixture will blend it in quickly and smoothly.

Beating egg whites

The airy, sponge-like, texture of a cold soufflé is achieved by the careful addition of egg whites. They must be beaten until stiff, but not dry, to enable them to be mixed in easily.

Gently fold egg whites into a mousse, or soufflé mixture with a large metal spoon, or rubber spatula. Cut through the center of the mixture, right down to the bottom of the mixing bowl, then bring the mixture up and over itself. Give the bowl a quarter turn, and repeat. Repeat until completely mixed in. Pour into the dish.

Soufflé dishes and molds

Choose a soufflé dish that is about 2½–3 inches deep; the mixture will rise above the dish by up to as much as half the depth of the dish. If you are using a larger quantity of mixture, use a wider dish, rather than a deeper one.

For a cold soufflé to be set above the dish, the dish must have a paper collar put around it. Wax paper or baking parchment can be used. Cut a length of paper long enough to fit around the dish, with an overlap. The width of the paper strip should be 2–2½ inches wider than the depth of the souffle dish. Place the strip around the dish and secure it with tape.

Molds, for molded desserts, should have a clearly defined pattern. Tin-lined copper are usually the best molds; it is also easier to remove a set mixture from a metal mold than from a thick china, or glass mold. When the mold is dipped into hot water, the heat will penetrate quickly through metal, melting the mixture sufficiently for it to slide out easily. Molds may be lightly oiled with a little almond oil, but never with a cooking oil as this could taint the delicate flavor of the cream.

Frozen Passion Fruit Soufflé

A velvety smooth soufflé to make the perfect ending to a dinner party, it should be made the day before. The soufflé can be decorated with whipped cream and pistachio nuts, but as its impressive qualities are in the texture and fresh flavor, it really doesn't need to be dressed-up.

16 passion fruit	2½ cups heavy cream
6 egg yolks	
1 cup sugar	SERVES EIGHT

Prepare a 6 inch diameter, 3 inch deep, soufflé dish as instructed on page 68.

Cut each passion fruit in half and scoop out the flesh and seeds into a nylon sieve placed over a small bowl then press with a spoon to extract all of the juice – about ⅔ cup.

Put the egg yolks into a large bowl and beat well until very thick.

Put 4 tablespoons of the passion fruit juice into a small saucepan with the sugar. Stir over a low heat until the sugar has dissolved, then bring to the boil and boil until the temperature reaches 230° on a candy thermometer. Beat the syrup in a steady stream into the egg yolks, then continue beating until the mixture cools and thickens. Gradually beat in the remaining passion fruit juice, beating until the mixture is thick and mousse-like.

Whip the cream until it just holds its shape. Fold the cream into the passion fruit mixture until no trace of white remains. Pour into the prepared soufflé dish, then freeze until firm. Once frozen, cover the top of the soufflé with plastic wrap.

To serve, remove the soufflé from the freezer 20–30 minutes before serving and carefully peel off the plastic wrap and paper. Serve the soufflé on a doily-lined dish.

Simple Lemon Soufflé

This simple soufflé is the lightest and most refreshing of all cold soufflés and is a perfect palate freshener.

6 eggs, separated
1 cup sugar
finely grated rind and
  juice of 3 large lemons
5½ teaspoons unflavored
  gelatin
¼ cup water

Decoration
¾ cup heavy cream
2 teaspoons sugar
finely grated lemon rind

SERVES SIX

Prepare a 6 inch diameter, 3 inch deep, soufflé dish as instructed on page 68.

Beat the egg yolks, sugar and lemon rind in a large bowl, until very thick, and the mixture holds the trail of the beater for at least 5 seconds. Gradually beat in the strained lemon juice.

Sprinkle the gelatin over the water in a small bowl and leave to soften for 2 minutes. Stand in a pan of hot water and stir until dissolved and hot.

Beat the egg whites until stiff, but not dry. Whisk the gelatin into the lemon mixture, then carefully fold in the egg whites until no trace of white remains.

Pour the soufflé mixture into the prepared dish, then cut through the surface of the soufflé with a small pointed knife, to level. Chill until set.

Whip the cream with the sugar until it is just thick enough to pipe, then spoon into a pastry bag fitted with a small star tip. Carefully peel off the paper collar from the soufflé. Decorate with rosettes of cream, then sprinkle with lemon rind.

Chocolate and Orange Mousse

Serve this mousse in tall glasses. It is very rich, so choose it as a dessert for a menu where the main course is not rich.

6 oz semi-sweet chocolate
2 tablespoons orange
  juice
finely grated rind of
  1 orange
3 tablespoons unsalted
  butter
4 eggs, separated
1 cup heavy cream

3 tablespoons
  confectioners' sugar
1–2 tablespoons Grand
  Marnier, or brandy

Decoration
grated chocolate curls
finely grated orange rind

SERVES SIX

Break up the chocolate and put in a large bowl with the orange juice and rind. Set the bowl over a saucepan of hot water until the chocolate melts, stirring frequently. Add the butter, a little at a time, then stir in the egg yolks. Remove the bowl from the heat.

Beat the egg whites until stiff, but not dry, then fold them into the chocolate mixture. Divide the mixture evenly between six tall glasses and chill until set.

Whip the cream with the confectioners' sugar and the Grand Marnier until it just holds soft peaks. Spoon the cream in whirls on top of the mousse. Decorate with chocolate curls and grated orange rind. Serve well chilled.

STRAWBERRY BAVAROIS (page 74)

Raspberry Soufflé

Frozen raspberries may be used when fresh ones are not available. Other purées, such as strawberry, apricot, blackberry, black currant, blueberry or mango may be used instead of raspberry.

½ lb raspberries
6 eggs, separated
⅔ cup sugar
1½ tablespoons
  unflavored powdered
  gelatin
¼ cup water
¾ cup heavy cream

Decoration
¾ cup heavy cream,
  whipped
fresh raspberries

SERVES SIX TO EIGHT

Prepare a 6 inch diameter, 3 inch deep, soufflé dish as instructed on page 68. Press the raspberries through a nylon sieve to make a purée.

Beat the egg yolks and sugar in a large bowl, until pale and thick and the mixture holds the trail of the beater for at least 5 seconds. Beat in the purée.

Sprinkle the gelatin over the water in a small bowl and leave to soften for 2 minutes. Stand in a saucepan of hot water and stir until dissolved and very hot.

Whip the cream until it will hold soft peaks. Beat the egg whites until stiff, but not dry.

Whisk the gelatin into the raspberry mixture. Fold in the cream, then the egg whites. Pour the mixture into the prepared soufflé dish and level the surface. Chill until set.

Carefully peel off the paper from the soufflé. Decorate the top of the soufflé with whipped cream and fresh raspberries.

Crème Brûlée

Crème brûlée is a specialty of Trinity College, Cambridge University. The split vanilla bean used for flavoring gives the custard a speckled appearance; if preferred, ¼ teaspoon vanilla extract can be used instead.

8 egg yolks
⅓ cup sugar
2½ cups heavy cream

1 vanilla bean, split
  lengthwise or
¼ teaspoon vanilla
  extract

SERVES FOUR TO SIX

Put the egg yolks into a mixing bowl with half of the sugar and whisk very lightly together.

Put the cream into a saucepan with the vanilla bean and heat gently until almost boiling. Gently whisk the cream into the egg yolks.

Set the bowl of custard over a saucepan of hot water and cook, stirring, until the custard becomes thick. Immediately, stir in the vanilla extract, if using, then strain the custard through a nylon sieve into a heatproof serving dish, about 8 inches diameter and 1 inch deep. Allow the custard to cool, then chill in the refrigerator, preferably overnight, until set.

About 2 hours before serving, remove the custard from the refrigerator and sprinkle the surface with the remaining sugar, making sure that it forms a very even layer. Allow to stand for about 10 minutes, then place under a hot broiler until the sugar dissolves and turns a golden caramel color. Cool, then chill before serving.

Blackberry Mousse

This mousse is made without gelatin and must be chilled thoroughly before serving. It can also be made with raspberries or strawberries.

½ lb fresh or frozen blackberries	a few blackberries, with leaves if possible, to decorate
2 eggs, separated	
⅓ cup sugar	
1¼ cups heavy cream	SERVES SIX

Press the blackberries through a nylon sieve to make a purée, about 1 cup.

Beat the egg yolks in a large mixing bowl with the sugar until very thick, then beat in the blackberry purée.

Whip the cream until thick enough to leave a trail on the surface when the beater is lifted, then fold into the blackberry mixture. Continue to beat until the mixture will form a heavy trail. Beat the egg whites until they stand in soft peaks, then fold into the blackberry mixture.

Spoon the blackberry mousse into six stem glasses and chill for about 2 hours. Serve decorated with fresh blackberries and their leaves, hung in clusters over the sides of the glasses.

Old English Syllabub

Bring out the full fragrance of the spices by grinding them just before you use them. Decorate the syllabub with fresh edible flower petals such as nasturtium, geranium, and rose, or with borage flowers.

1 clove	6 tablespoons pale cream sherry
1 allspice berry	
1 inch piece of cinnamon stick	1¼ cups heavy cream
a little freshly grated nutmeg	24 amaretti cookies
⅓ cup sugar	
finely grated rind and juice of 1 lemon	SERVES FOUR

Put the clove, allspice and cinnamon stick into a small mortar and grind very finely, then sift through a fine sieve.

Put the ground spices, nutmeg, sugar, lemon rind, and strained lemon juice into a bowl with the sherry. Stir well until the sugar dissolves, then cover and leave to stand for 1 hour.

Strain the sherry mixture through a fine nylon sieve into a clean bowl. Pour in the cream in a steady stream, beating all the time. Continue beating the mixture until it is just thick enough to hold the trail of the beater.

Place four cookies in each of four serving glasses, then fill each glass with the spicy syllabub. Chill for about 1 hour. Decorate with the remaining cookies and a few fresh flower petals.

Coeurs à la Crème

These pretty heart-shaped creams are traditionally served with wild strawberries, but they can also be served with other fresh, sharp-flavored fruits such as raspberries, strawberries or sliced kiwi fruit.

1¼ cups small-curd cottage cheese or ricotta cheese
3 tablespoons sugar
finely grated rind of 1 lemon
finely grated rind of 1 orange
1¼ cups heavy cream
2 egg whites

Decoration
¾ cup heavy cream
wild strawberries, raspberries or kiwi fruit, to serve

SERVES SIX

Rinse 12 pieces of cheesecloth in water and wring out well. Line six coeur à la crème molds with a double layer of cheesecloth, pressing it well into the corners, allowing the cloth to overhang the edges.

Sieve the cheese through a nylon sieve into a bowl, then mix in the sugar and the rind.

Whip the cream until it will hold soft peaks. Beat the egg whites until stiff, but not dry. Fold the cream into the cheese, then fold in the whites.

Spoon the cheese mixture into the molds, then bring the cloth up and over the filling. Place on a plate and leave to drain overnight in the refrigerator.

Discard all the collected liquid and invert the creams carefully onto individual serving plates and gently remove the cheesecloth. Pour the heavy cream evenly over the hearts, then decorate with the chosen fruit.

Lime Syllabub

Serve this well-flavored syllabub with langues de chat cookies. Lemon may be used instead of lime, but if so, use only one.

thinly pared rind and juice of 3 limes
⅔ cup white wine
2 tablespoons brandy
½ cup sugar

1¼ cups heavy cream
lime twists, to decorate

SERVES FOUR TO SIX

Put the lime rind and juice, white wine, brandy and sugar into a bowl. Stir well until the sugar has dissolved, then cover and let stand for about 2 hours.

Remove the rind from the wine with a slotted spoon and discard. Pour the cream into the wine in a continuous stream, beating constantly. Continue beating the mixture until thick and it holds the trail of the beater, then pour into stem glasses and chill. Serve decorated with lime twists.

Petits Pots de Crème – Caramel

Care must be taken when making the caramel; should it become too dark it will give the cream a bitter flavor. You can use all milk instead of milk and cream, if preferred.

½ cup sugar	1 whole egg
3 tablespoons water	1¼ cups heavy cream
1¼ cups milk	
5 egg yolks	SERVES SIX TO EIGHT

Put the sugar into a heavy-based saucepan with the water and heat gently until the sugar has dissolved.

Bring the sugar syrup to a boil and boil until it turns a light brown caramel color, then immediately plunge the base of the saucepan into cold water to stop the caramel cooking and darkening further. Carefully pour in the milk, then heat gently until the caramel dissolves into the milk.

Lightly whisk the egg yolks and whole egg together. Stir in the cream, and the caramel-flavored milk. Strain the mixture through a nylon sieve into eight ⅓-cup petit pots, or six ½-cup soufflé dishes. Cover with lids or small rounds of foil.

Stand the dishes on a trivet in a large, wide saucepan, and add enough boiling water to come about halfway up the sides of the dishes. Cover the pan with a lid, then steam the creams over a gentle heat for 15–20 minutes until they are very lightly set. Allow to cool. Chill well before serving.

Petits Pots de Crème – Chocolate

If you do not have the special little china pots for making this rich cream, you can use small soufflé dishes or ramekins. A less rich cream can be made by using milk instead of cream.

2½ cups heavy cream	1 whole egg
½ teaspoon vanilla extract	3 tablespoons sugar
6 oz semi-sweet chocolate, broken into small pieces	SERVES SIX TO EIGHT
5 egg yolks	

Put the cream, vanilla extract and the chocolate into a saucepan and heat gently, stirring, until the chocolate melts and the mixture becomes smooth.

Lightly mix the egg yolks, whole egg and the sugar together, then stir in the chocolate cream. Strain the mixture through a nylon sieve into eight ⅓-cup petit pots, or six ½-cup soufflé dishes. Cover the petit pots with lids or small rounds of foil; cover the soufflé dishes with foil.

Stand the dishes on a trivet in a large, wide saucepan, and add enough boiling water to come about halfway up the sides of the dishes. Cover the pan with a lid, then steam the creams over a gently heat for 15–20 minutes until they are very lightly set. Remove from the pan and allow to cool. Chill well before serving.

Vanilla Bavarian Ring

This vanilla-flavored bavarois is set in a ring mold and decorated with chocolate leaves, but it can be set in any pretty mold and decorated with cherries or grapes dipped in caramel; piped chocolate scrolls; fresh fruits, or edible flower petals.

1 tablespoon unflavored
  gelatin
3 tablespoons water
6 egg yolks
⅓ cup sugar
2½ cups light cream
1 teaspoon vanilla extract

Decoration
3 oz semi-sweet chocolate
12 rose leaves
¾ cup crème Chantilly
  (see page 94)

SERVES SIX

Sprinkle the gelatin over the water and leave to soften while making the custard.

Lightly whisk the egg yolks and 1¼ cups sugar together in a bowl. Bring the cream and the vanilla extract almost to a boil, then whisk into the egg yolks. Set the bowl over a saucepan of hot water and cook the custard, stirring, until it thickens enough to coat the back of the spoon (alternatively, cook in a microwave oven on full power for 2–2½ minutes, stirring every 30 seconds with a wire whisk).

Strain the custard through a nylon sieve into a clean bowl and add the gelatin. Stir until it is completely dissolved. Allow the custard to cool, stirring frequently to prevent a skin forming.

Whip the remaining heavy cream until it will just hold soft peaks, then fold the custard and the cream together. Pour into a 1-quart ring mold. Chill until set.

Meanwhile, make the decoration. Melt the chocolate and dip the underside of the rose leaves into the chocolate. Leave to set, then remove leaves.

To unmold the bavarois, quickly dip the mold, right up to the rim, into hot water. Place a serving plate on top, then invert the mold.

Whip the crème Chantilly until thick enough to pipe, then fill a pastry bag fitted with a star tip. Pipe the cream around the base of the mold, then decorate with the chocolate leaves.

Strawberry Bavarois

It is essential to use really well-flavored strawberries for this bavarois – frozen strawberries may be used, but only as a last resort.

about ¾ lb fresh
  strawberries
1½ tablespoons
  unflavored gelatin
¼ cup water
6 egg yolks
⅓ cup sugar
1¼ cups milk
1¼ cups heavy cream

Strawberry sauce
½ lb fresh strawberries

⅓ cup sugar
1 tablespoon framboise
  liqueur, optional

Decoration
¾ cup heavy cream,
  whipped
fresh strawberries

SERVES SIX TO EIGHT

Press the strawberries through a very fine nylon sieve to make a purée, about 1¼ cups.

Sprinkle the gelatin over the water in a small bowl and leave to soften while making the custard.

Lightly whisk the egg yolks and the sugar together. Bring the milk almost to a boil, then whisk it into the egg yolks. Set the bowl over a saucepan of hot water, and cook the custard, stirring, until it thickens enough to coat the back of the spoon (alternatively, cook in a microwave oven on full power for 2½–3 minutes, stirring every 30 seconds with a wire whisk).

Strain the custard through a nylon sieve into a clean bowl and add the gelatin, stirring until it is completely dissolved. Set the custard aside until cold, but not set, stirring frequently to prevent a skin from forming.

Whip the cream until it will just hold soft peaks. Stir the strawberry purée into the custard, then gently fold into the whipped cream. Pour the mixture into a 1½-quart mold. Chill until set.

Meanwhile, make the sauce: slice the strawberries and put them into a bowl. Sprinkle with the sugar and the liqueur, if using. Cover and leave to stand for about 1 hour, then press through a nylon sieve to form a purée. Pour into a serving pitcher and chill.

To unmold the bavarois, quickly dip the mold, right up to the rim, into hot water. Place a serving plate on top, then invert the mold and the plate together, giving the mold a sharp shake to free the bavarois. Decorate with whipped cream and fresh strawberries. Serve with the strawberry sauce.

Meringues

THE MOST frequently asked cookery question must be "Why can't I make meringue?" a fact that would surely sadden its Swiss creator, a pastry chef called Gasparini, who was said to have created it as long ago as 1720.

Meringue can be used to make simple piped shells that can be dipped into chocolate, sprinkled with nuts, or sandwiched together with flavorful creams. It makes a fluffy, light topping for pies and puddings; elaborate cakes; nests and baskets for filling with fruits and creams; or it can become a grand presentation in the form of a meringue Croquembouche.

◆ Making Meringue ◆

The egg whites must be beaten in a clean bowl until they are very stiff, and will hold an unwavering peak on the end of the whisk or beater. They must remain smooth, and not break up.

The sugar can be added in two ways. Half the sugar can be beaten in, then the remaining half folded in, taking care not to overfold and break down the egg whites. This meringue can be piped, but it is better for spooning on top of pies, or for baked Alaska. Alternatively, all the sugar may be beaten in, a little at a time, beating well after each addition. This makes a very smooth, shiny meringue for piping.

Meringue cuite (literally meaning cooked) is made by putting the unbeaten whites and granulated or confectioners' sugar into a large mixing bowl, then beating them over gently simmering water until they become stiff and thick. As soon as the mixture becomes thick, the bowl should be removed from the heat, and the meringue beaten until it will hold stiff peaks. This meringue has a smooth texture and a wonderful gloss. It is perfect for piping as it keeps a clearly defined shape. However, care must be taken not to overheat the meringue when beating, or it will form a frothy, cooked egg texture.

Once made, meringue should be used immediately. If it is left for any length of time it will collapse, become watery, and be unusable. Meringue can be baked in the oven at a very low temperature for a long time to completely dry out (as for shells, disks, and nests) or it can be baked at a higher temperature for a short time – just long enough to set the outside, and brown it, while the center remains very soft.

◆ Drying Meringues ◆

How meringues are cooked is very much a personal choice, but it seems that everyone's ideal is to dry them out so that they remain pure white. This is for visual effect only. Creamy colored meringues with a slightly soft center have a better flavor, but they don't look quite so attractive.

For meringues to remain pure white, they need to be left in an oven set at its lowest possible setting, for several hours, even overnight in some cases. Check from time to time to make sure that they are not coloring.

LEMON MERINGUE PIE (page 79)

Meringue Medley

Made with meringue cuite, these little meringues are favorites with adults and children alike. Serve with morning coffee, or afternoon tea.

6 egg whites	¼ cup (1 oz) finely
2 cups sugar	chopped pecans,
1 tablespoon finely	walnuts, or hazelnuts,
chopped pistachio nuts	1 tablespoon raspberry
1¼ cups heavy cream	jam
1 tablespoon Grand	3 oz semi-sweet
Marnier	chocolate, melted

MAKES FORTY-FOUR SMALL
MERINGUES

Line several baking sheets with baking parchment paper.

Put the egg whites and sugar in a large bowl over a large saucepan of hot water and beat until very stiff and shiny. Remove from the heat and continue beating until the meringue will hold unwavering peaks – on no account let the meringue become too hot.

Fill a large pastry bag, fitted with a large star tip, with meringue and pipe out as follows:

To make whirls: pipe 24 whirls of meringue on the lined baking sheets, about 1½ inches in diameter.

To make oblong spirals: pipe the meringue in a spiral fashion to make 24 spirals about 3 inches long. Or, if you find it easier, pipe a joined line of shells to the same length.

To make pistachio fingers: simply pipe 20 straight lines of meringue about 3 inches long on the baking sheets, then sprinkle with chopped pistachio nuts.

Bake the meringues in a preheated 275° oven for

2–2½ hours, or until completely dried out. Change the sheets around in the oven during cooking, to ensure that they all dry evenly. Allow the meringues to cool, then remove from the paper and complete as follows or store in an airtight tin until required.

Whirls: whip ⅔ cup of the cream with the Grand Marnier until it will hold soft peaks, then fold in the chopped nuts. Sandwich the meringues together, in pairs, with the nut cream, then place in small paper cases for serving.

Spirals: whip the remaining cream until thick, then fold in the raspberry jam. Put the cream into a pastry bag fitted with a large star tip. Sandwich the meringues together, in pairs, with piped cream. Put the meringues into small paper cases for serving.

Pistachio fingers: dip the base of each meringue in the melted chocolate to coat it evenly, removing excess chocolate by gently pulling the meringue across the back of a knife. Place on wax paper until set.

Lemon Meringue Pie

Lemon meringue pie comes in various forms.
This delicious version has a lemon filling which
is cool, smooth and tangy.

1 quantity pâte sucrée (see page 92)	⅓–½ cup sugar
lightly whipped cream, to serve	3 egg yolks
Filling	*Meringue*
rind and juice of 4 large lemons	3 egg whites
2½ cups water	1 cup sugar
½ cup cornstarch	SERVES SIX TO EIGHT

Roll out the pâte sucrée on a lightly floured surface to a round 1 inch larger than a 9-inch fluted tart pan or pie pan. Line the pan with the pastry, pressing it well into the flutes. Trim the edge, then prick the pastry well, all over, with a fork. Chill for 30 minutes, then bake blind in a preheated 425° oven for 25–30 minutes, until cooked and lightly browned. Allow to cool. Leave the oven on.

Meanwhile, prepare the filling, put the lemon rind in a saucepan with the water, bring to a boil, then remove from the heat, cover, and leave to stand for at least 30 minutes.

Remove all of the lemon rind from the pan, then stir in the lemon juice. Blend the cornstarch with a little of the lemon liquid to form a smooth paste, pour it into the pan and stir well. Bring the lemon mixture to a boil, stirring continuously. Reduce the heat and continue cooking until every trace of raw cornstarch disappears, and the mixture has thickened. Stir in the sugar to taste, adding a little more if liked, then beat in the egg yolks. Pour the lemon filling into the pastry case.

To make the meringue, beat the egg whites until stiff, but not dry, then gradually beat in the sugar, adding a little at a time and beating well between each addition, until the meringue is very stiff and shiny. Put the meringue into a large pastry bag fitted with a large star tip, then pipe it attractively on top of the lemon filling.

Alternatively, spoon the meringue onto the filling and shape it into swirls with a long narrow spatula. Bake for 5–10 minutes until the meringue is very lightly browned. Remove the pie from the oven and allow to cool, then refrigerate until quite cold.

Swiss Tart

The tip of every meringue star in this dessert is dotted with a bead of red currant jelly to give a jeweled effect. A little skill with a pastry bag is needed as each star must have a clean point, to enable it to be dotted with jelly.

1 quantity of pâte sucrée
   (see page 92)

Filling
1⅓ cups sugar
juice of 1 lemon, strained
¾ cup water
2 lb apples

Meringue
3 egg whites
1 cup sugar
2 tablespoons red currant
   jelly or seedless
   raspberry jelly

SERVES SIX TO EIGHT

Roll the pâte sucrée out on a lightly floured surface to a round 1 inch larger than a 9-inch fluted tart pan. Line the pan with the pastry, pressing it well into the flutes. Trim the edge, then prick the pastry well, all over, with a fork. Chill for 30 minutes.

Bake blind in a preheated 425° oven for 20–25 minutes until cooked, and lightly browned. Allow to cool. Reduce the oven temperature to 275°.

To make the filling, put the sugar and lemon juice into a wide saucepan with the water. Heat gently until the sugar has dissolved, then bring to a boil gently for 5 minutes. Peel, quarter, core and slice the apples, cutting the slices about ¼ inch thick. Add the apple slices, in batches, to the sugar syrup and poach until just tender. Lift out with a slotted spoon and drain well on paper towels.

Leaving the pastry case in the tart pan, arrange the apple slices neatly inside the pastry case.

Put the egg whites and the sugar for the meringue into a bowl, then place over a pan of hot water. Beat until stiff, remove from the heat and continue beating until the meringue forms unwavering peaks. Put into a pastry bag fitted with a large star tip, then pipe stars over the top of the apple-filled tart, making sure that each star is finished with a clean point. Continue to pipe the meringue, in decreasing circles, until it builds up to a point.

Bake for 1 hour until the meringue is set, but not browned – it must remain as white as possible.

Put the red currant jelly into a small paper pastry bag and cut a small hole in the bottom of the bag. Pipe a small bead of jelly on the tip of every meringue star. Serve the tart warm or cold.

SWISS TART (above)

Meringue and Ganache Cake

This very rich cake makes a lovely party-time special.

4 egg whites	2–3 tablespoons Grand
1⅓ cups sugar	Marnier, brandy or rum
12 oz semi-sweet	confectioners' sugar for
chocolate	sifting
2 cups heavy cream	
	SERVES FOURTEEN TO
	SIXTEEN

Line four baking sheets with baking parchment paper. Draw an 8-inch circle in the center of each sheet of paper.

Beat the egg whites until stiff, but not dry, then gradually beat in the sugar, a little at a time, beating well until the meringue is very stiff and shiny. Divide the meringue equally between the four baking sheets, then spread evenly to form neat rounds. Bake in a preheated 275° oven for 1–1¼ hours until dry, swapping over the baking sheets during cooking to ensure that they dry evenly. Cool.

Meanwhile, break the chocolate into small pieces and put into a large saucepan with the cream. Heat gently, stirring, until the chocolate melts and blends with the cream to form a smooth rich cream; do not allow to boil.

Pour the cream into a mixing bowl and leave to cool, stirring frequently to prevent a skin forming. When the chocolate cream is cold, add the Grand Marnier and beat well until light and fluffy – do not overwhip as the cream will turn buttery.

Place one of the meringue layers on a flat serving plate, then spread with a generous layer of the whipped chocolate cream. Continue until the meringue rounds are sandwiched together.

Spread the remaining chocolate cream all over the meringue to cover completely. Mark the cream into swirls with a palette knife. Sift confectioners' sugar lightly over the cake. Refrigerate the cake until it is slightly chilled, but do not let the chocolate cream set too hard. Serve the cake still slightly chilled, so the chocolate cream is still firm.

Hazelnut Meringue Cake

This simple cake is perfect for the novice meringue-maker. The sharp flavor of the raspberries contrasts well with the nutty meringue.

3 egg whites	confectioners' sugar for
1 cup sugar	sifting
½ cup (2 oz) hazelnuts,	finely chopped pistachio
skinned, toasted and	nuts for sprinkling
finely chopped	
1¼ cups heavy cream	SERVES SIX TO EIGHT
¾ lb fresh raspberries,	
hulled	

Line two baking sheets with baking parchment paper, then draw 8 inch circle in the center of each piece of paper.

Beat the egg whites until they are very stiff, but not dry. Adding just a little sugar at a time, gradually beat the sugar into the egg whites, beating well between each addition until the meringue is stiff and very shiny. Carefully fold in the chopped hazelnuts.

Divide the meringue equally between the two baking sheets, then spread neatly into rounds. With a long narrow spatula, mark the top of one of the rounds into swirls – this will be the top meringue. Bake in a preheated oven 275° oven for about

1½ hours until dry. Turn the oven off, and allow the meringues to cool in the oven.

Whip the cream until it will hold soft peaks. Carefully remove the meringues from the baking paper. Place the smooth meringue round on a large flat serving plate, then spread with the cream. Arrange the raspberries on top of the cream, then place the second meringue on top. Sift confectioners' sugar over the top of the cake, and sprinkle with finely chopped pistachio nuts. Serve the cake as soon as possible.

Tropical Pavlova

Originally created for the Russian dancer Anna Pavlova, this delicious meringue cake with its marshmallow-like center is served here with a fruit filling.

4 egg whites	1 teaspoon vanilla extract
¾ teaspoon cream of tartar	1 ripe mango, peeled and diced
1⅓ cups sugar	2 kiwi fruits, peeled and sliced
1 teaspoon white vinegar	
1 teaspoon vanilla extract	2 slices of fresh pineapple, peeled, cored and diced
2 teaspoons cornstarch	
Decoration	
2 cups heavy cream	SERVES SIX TO EIGHT

Line a large baking sheet with baking parchment paper. Beat the egg whites with the cream of tartar until stiff, but not dry. Gradually beat in the sugar, then quickly beat in the vinegar, vanilla and cornstarch.

Spoon the meringue into the center of the lined baking sheet. Using a large narrow spatula, spread the meringue to form a smooth oval shape, about 9 inches long and 1½ inches deep. Bake in a preheated 275° oven for 1¼ hours. Turn the heat off and leave the meringue in the oven until quite dry.

Transfer the meringue to a serving plate, carefully peeling off the paper. Whip the cream with the vanilla until stiff, then spoon into a pastry bag fitted with a medium-sized star tip. Pipe shells of cream around the outer edge of the Pavlova. Pipe a second outer, inner ring of cream, leaving a gap two inches between. Fill the gap with the prepared fruits. (If preferred, the cream may be spread on top of the Pavlova, with the fruits arranged in the center.)

Meringue Nests

Once these little nests have been well dried out they may be stored in an airtight tin almost indefinitely, making them invaluable as a stand-by in the pantry, for instant desserts and unexpected visitors. This recipe gives two alternative fillings (each enough to fill 12 nests), but they can be more simply filled with whipped cream and fruit, or with ice cream.

---

5 egg whites	¾ cup small-curd cottage
1⅔ cups sugar	cheese, sieved
	¾ cup heavy cream
Cranberry filling	
2 tablespoons cornstarch	*Chestnut filling*
1¼ cups milk	2 cups heavy cream
⅔ cup sugar	1 teaspoon vanilla extract
½ lb cranberries or	1 lb can sweetened
blueberries	chestnut purée
¼ cup water	grated chocolate curls, to
2 teaspoons arrowroot	decorate

MAKES TWELVE NESTS

Line two baking sheets with baking parchment paper. Draw twelve 4-inch circles on the paper.

Beat the egg whites until they are very stiff, but not dry, then gradually beat in the sugar a little at a time, beating well after each addition, until the meringue is very stiff and shiny.

Put the meringue into a large pastry bag fitted with a medium-sized star tip. Fill in each drawn circle on the baking paper, with a continuous spiral of meringue. Pipe stars of meringue around the edge of each meringue base to form a little wall. Bake in a preheated 200° oven for 4–5 hours. Turn the oven off and leave the meringues in the oven until cool.

For berry-filled nests, blend the cornstarch with 1 tablespoon of the sugar and a little of the milk to form a smooth paste. Bring the remaining milk to a boil, then stir it into the cornstarch mixture. Return the custard to the saucepan and cook over a low heat, stirring, until the custard thickens. Pour the custard into a clean bowl, then cover the surface closely with plastic wrap to prevent a skin forming. Allow to cool, then refrigerate until quite cold.

Put the berries into a saucepan with the remaining sugar and water, cover and cook gently for about 15 minutes until the berries are softened. Blend the arrowroot with a little cold water to form a smooth paste, then stir into the cranberries. Bring to a boil, stirring until the mixture thickens and clears. Pour into a small bowl, cover the surface closely with plastic wrap to prevent a skin forming, allow to cool, then refrigerate until well chilled.

Beat the cottage cheese until it is soft and smooth. Whip the cream until it will hold soft peaks. Whisk the cold custard until it is very smooth, mix with the cottage cheese, then fold in the cream. Divide the custard mixture between the meringue nests, then spoon the cranberries on top. Serve immediately, or chill until ready to serve.

For chestnut filled nests, whip the cream with the vanilla extract until it is just thick enough to pipe, then put it into a pastry bag fitted with a medium-sized star tip.

Spoon the chestnut purée into the meringue nests, then pipe the cream in whirls on top. If preferred, the cream may be spooned on top. Sprinkle chocolate curls over the cream. Serve immediately, or chill until ready to serve.

HAZELNUT MERINGUE CAKE (page 82)

Basic Recipes

SURPRISINGLY few pieces of special equipment are needed to create wonderful cakes and pastries. Large heavy baking sheets are essential, as is a pastry bag with a good selection of plain and star tips. A torten ring is most useful, and is a good buy if you don't already have one. This is a deep metal ring that can be expanded, or reduced, to whatever size you wish. It can also be used as a mold for baking sponge cakes, by placing it on a foil-lined baking sheet, with the foil pleated up around the ring to prevent the batter seeping out. But the rings are particularly useful for assembling layered cakes. The ring enables the cake to be trimmed to an exact size, and it keeps the layers held firmly together while being assembled, to give a perfect shape when finished. Springform pans are useful and should have a good solid base; some have very thin bases that become very wavy, which in turn can make cakes very uneven. The measurements for all of the pans and dishes used throughout this book are taken across the top.

Baking parchment paper, and wax paper are both essential for lining pans, and for making disposable paper pastry bags. Several sizes of long narrow spatulas with very flexible blades are useful.

Génoise

This very light sponge cake is the foundation for many cakes, but it can also be used to make quick cakes for afternoon tea, or for desserts.

Although Génoise can be used on the same day it is made, it is much easier to handle, and will cut better, if it is kept for a day, well wrapped in plastic wrap or foil before using. Génoise becomes more moist with keeping, and will keep well for two or three days. It also freezes well.

The eggs and sugar are normally beaten in a bowl over a saucepan of gently simmering water with a balloon whisk, rotary beater, or hand held electric mixer – but if you have a large free standing mixer, beating over hot water is unnecessary.

To achieve a very light sponge, use a large metal spoon or a rubber spatula to fold in the flour as these enable you to cut cleanly through the beaten egg mixture without losing any of the air. Always make sure that the melted butter is quite cool before adding it to the sponge mixture; if it is too hot it will deflate the mixture. As soon as the last trace of butter disappears, pour the mixture into a prepared pan and bake immediately – if the mixture is left to stand for any length of time it will simply collapse and be unusable.

6 eggs
1 cup sugar
1⅓ cups cake flour

6 tablespoons unsalted
    butter, melted and
    cooled

MAKES A 10-inch CAKE

Butter and lightly flour a 10-inch round springform pan. Line the bottom with a round of wax paper.

Put the eggs and sugar into a large bowl, place over a saucepan of hot water and beat well until the mixture becomes very thick, and very light in color. Remove from the heat and beat until cold, and thick enough to leave a trail on the surface when the beater is lifted. Alternatively, beat the eggs and sugar together in a large electric mixer until they hold a trail almost indefinitely.

Sift the flour into a bowl, then gradually fold into the beaten mixture, cutting through and folding the mixture over to incorporate the flour, turning the bowl each time you cut through the mixture. Fold in the cooled butter a little at a time, taking care not to overmix or the mixture will collapse.

Pour the batter into the prepared pan, tapping the pan gently to level the batter. Bake in a preheated 350° oven for 40–45 minutes until the sponge is well risen, firm to the touch, and has shrunk very slightly away from the side of the pan. Cool the sponge in the pan for about 10 minutes, then transfer to a wire rack to cool completely.

Biscuit de Savoie

This light, fatless sponge is made with potato flour. As with Génoise, the sponge will contract as it cools. If it dips in the center, simply trim the sides to level.

6 tablespoons potato flour
6 tablespoons cake flour
5 eggs, separated
1 cup sugar

finely grated rind of
    1 lemon

MAKES A 10-inch CAKE

Butter and lightly flour a 10 inch round springform pan. Line the bottom with a round of wax paper.

Sift the flour together twice. Beat the egg yolks with three-quarters of the sugar and lemon rind in a large mixing bowl until they are very thick.

Beat the egg whites until stiff, but not dry, then gradually beat in the remaining sugar, beating until very shiny. Carefully fold the sifted flours into the egg yolk mixture, then gradually fold in the egg whites.

Pour the sponge batter into the prepared pan and bake in a preheated 350° oven for 40–45 minutes until very well risen, and a wooden toothpick or skewer inserted in the center of the sponge comes out clean. Allow the sponge to cool in the pan for 10 minutes, then transfer to a wire rack to cool completely.

Basic Pie Pastry

Although this is the simplest and most basic of all pastries, it requires a cool, very light hand to obtain a good result. All-purpose flour should always be used. The fat can be butter, margarine, or a mixture of butter and margarine, and shortening. The addition of shortening helps to make a much shorter (crumblier) texture, but butter will certainly make the best flavored pastry.

This pastry is bound together with chilled water and care must be taken not to add too much, or too little. If the pastry is too wet, it will be sticky to handle and tough to eat. If it is too dry, it will crumble and be impossible to roll out. As flours vary in strength (the gluten content) from one brand to another, a little more or a little less water may be necessary to bind the mixture to the right consistency. The addition of sugar improves the flavor.

1½ cups all-purpose flour	6 tablespoons butter,
pinch of salt	cubed
1 tablespoon sugar	3–4 tablespoons chilled
	water

MAKES A 9″ PIE SHELL

Sift the flour, salt and sugar into a bowl. Rub in the butter until the mixture resembles fine bread crumbs.

Make a well in the center of the rubbed-in mixture, add the water and mix together with a round-bladed knife to form a dough that is firm and will leave the bowl quite clean. Turn the dough onto a lightly floured surface and knead it just for a few seconds until smooth. Use as directed.

Rich Pie Pastry

This richer version of basic pie pastry has a higher proportion of fat (which should be all butter or margarine) and an added egg yolk. It may also be made with a whole egg, instead of egg yolk and water. The pastry keeps well, and is excellent for pies or tarts that are to be eaten cold.

2 cups all-purpose flour	1 egg yolk
pinch of salt	3–4 tablespoons chilled
1 tablespoon sugar	water
12 tablespoons unsalted	
butter, cubed	MAKES A 9″ PIE SHELL

Sift the flour, salt and sugar into a bowl. Rub in the butter until the mixture resembles bread crumbs.

Mix the egg yolk and water together (this ensures an evenly colored pastry; when added separately the pastry can become streaky in appearance), add to the dough and mix lightly. Knead on a lightly floured surface for a few seconds until smooth.

Puff Pastry

Used to make famous pastries such as pithiver, mille-feuilles and jalousie, as well as numerous other large and small sweet pastries, this is one of the richest, and lightest pastries. Its lightness is achieved by the clever layering of a flour dough and butter, each layer being kept separate from the other, by air trapped between them as it is made.

Always use a good quality all-purpose flour, and a good firm butter, one that is neither too oily, nor too wet. Getting the amount of water right is most important. The dough needs to be soft and elastic, without being sticky, yet firm enough to contain the butter without letting it break through. If it is too dry it will be difficult to roll out and be tough.

When making puff pastry, it is essential to keep everything as cold as possible. The water should be well chilled, and the butter cold, but not so cold that it will be hard and break up, or break through the flour dough. Butter left at room temperature for about 15–20 minutes is usually just right by the time it has been beaten flat with a rolling pin.

Puff pastry is best eaten on the day it is made, otherwise it firms up and loses the light, flaky texture it has when freshly baked.

---

2 cups all-purpose flour
pinch of salt
½ lb (2 sticks) butter

1 tablespoon strained
    lemon juice
about ⅔ cup ice water

MAKES ABOUT 1 lb

Sift the flour and salt into a bowl. Lightly rub in 2 tablespoons of the butter.

Place the remaining butter between two sheets of wax paper and beat it out firmly with a rolling pin to form a smooth 6-inch square, then set aside.

Make a well in the center of the flour, add the lemon juice and iced water, then mix with a round-bladed knife to form a fairly soft, but not sticky dough. Place the dough on a lightly floured marble slab, or work surface, and, without kneading, roll out the dough to about a 10-inch square.

Place the square of butter in the center of the dough, so that it looks like a diamond shape. Bring each corner of the dough to the center of the butter, to enclose it completely, then turn the pastry 45 degrees to square it up.

Roll out the pastry to about 18 inches long, then take the bottom third of the pastry up and over the center third, bring the top third of the pastry down over the bottom third, trapping in as much air as you can between each layer as you do so. Press the edges firmly with the rolling pin to seal. Wrap the pastry in plastic wrap, put it on a plate and chill for 30 minutes. Do not leave the pastry in the refrigerator any longer than 30 minutes this will harden the butter and cause it to break up when you roll the pastry out again.

Remove the plastic wrap. Place the pastry on a lightly floured surface so that the short joined ends are at the top and the bottom. Roll out the pastry again to about 18 inches long. Fold into three once again, and seal. Brush off excess flour, then wrap and chill for another 30 minutes. Repeat this rolling out, and folding, process six more times, with a 30 minute rest between each one. Keep a note of how many times you have rolled the pastry – the simplest way to do this is to make small impressions in the pastry with your fingertips.

Now the pastry is ready to be used. Or, it may be frozen for up to 3 months.

Danish Pastry

Danish pastry, for making those celebrated Danish pastries, is made with a yeast dough enriched with butter, in a fashion very similar to puff pastry. The addition of yeast to the dough makes the pastry very light. The pastry does not require as many rollings and folding as does puff pastry, but all the basic rules for making puff pastry also apply to making Danish pastry.

2 cups all-purpose flour
pinch of salt
1 tablespoon sugar
½ lb (2 sticks) unsalted
   butter, at room
   temperature
1½ teaspoons active dry
   yeast and 1 teaspoon
   sugar

⅔ cup tepid water
1 egg, beaten

MAKES EIGHTEEN PASTRIES

Sift the flour, salt and sugar into a bowl, then rub in 2 tablespoons of the butter. Blend the yeast and sugar with the water.

Make a well in the center of the flour, add the yeast liquid and the egg. Mix to form a soft dough, then knead lightly on a floured surface for about 5 minutes until smooth. Put the dough inside a very lightly oiled plastic bag and chill for 10 minutes.

Meanwhile, place the remaining butter between two sheets of wax paper, or plastic wrap, and beat out firmly with a rolling pin to form a 6-inch square.

Remove the dough from the plastic bag and roll it out to about a 10-inch square. Place the square of butter in the center of the dough, so that it looks like a diamond shape, bring each corner of the dough to the center of the butter, enclosing it completely.

Turn the dough 45 degrees to make a square, then roll out the pastry to about 18 inches long. Take the bottom third of the pastry up and over the center third, then bring the top third of the pastry down over the bottom third. Press all the edges firmly with the rolling pin to seal. Put the pastry inside a lightly oiled plastic bag and chill for 10 minutes. Turning the pastry so that the short ends are at the top and bottom each time, repeat the rolling out, and folding into three, three more times with a 10 minute rest in between each one. Use as required.

The pastry will keep for 2–3 days in the refrigerator.

Choux Pastry

This light, airy pastry is used for many classic desserts, such as Croquembouche, Paris-Brest, and Gâteau Saint-Honoré. Due to the vast amount of air beaten into the pastry, it rises to four or five times its original size during baking, forming a hollow interior which is perfect for filling with flavored whipped creams, or crème pâtissière.
The secret of making light, crispy pastry is to take great care and not be too hasty when adding the beaten eggs. Thorough beating between each addition will ensure perfect results every time.
Choux pastry can be made very successfully by hand, but it is easier with a hand held electric mixer, or a large electric mixer.

¾ cup all-purpose flour
pinch of salt
7 tablespoons unsalted
  butter

1 cup cold water
3 eggs, beaten

MAKES ABOUT 1 lb

Sift the flour and the salt onto a small sheet of wax paper. Put the butter and water in a saucepan, heat very gently until the butter melts. Bring to a rolling boil. (Do not allow the water to boil before the butter melts, as this will evaporate off some of the water, and will in turn reduce the amount of liquid.)

Remove the pan from the heat and tip the flour into the boiling liquid, stirring it into the liquid as you do so. Return the pan to the heat, then beat the mixture just until it forms a ball, and leaves the sides of the pan; do not overbeat as the paste will become oily and separate.

Remove the pan from the heat and allow the paste to cool a little. Pour a little of the beaten eggs into the pan, then beat them into the paste. Continue to add the eggs, a little at a time, beating well between each addition, until they are all incorporated, and you have a very smooth shiny paste. Use and bake as directed in the individual recipes.

Pâte Sucrée

This is a very rich, sweet pastry, with an almost shortbread cookie-like texture. It is used mainly for making tart and tartlet cases. Because it has a high proportion of butter and sugar, it is a much softer pastry to use. In warm weather, it is best to chill it for half an hour before using. Traditionally, this pastry is made directly on a marble slab – the flour being sifted onto the slab and a well made in the center, into which are put the sugar, butter and egg yolks. The ingredients are then all gently worked together with the fingertips. However, equally good results are achieved by making the pastry in a mixing bowl, in the same way as rich pie pastry. Always use butter to ensure a good flavor.

1 cup all-purpose flour	6 tablespoons butter, cubed
pinch of salt	
⅓ cup confectioners' sugar	2 egg yolks

MAKES A 9″ PIE CRUST

Sift the flour, salt and confectioners' sugar into a bowl. Rub in the butter until the mixture resembles fine bread crumbs. Add the egg yolks and mix with a round-bladed knife to form a dough. Turn onto a lightly floured surface and knead for a few seconds until smooth.

Almond Pastry

Almond pastry is very similar to pâte sucrée, and is also used for tart and tartlet cases. Because it has the addition of ground almonds it is a very soft pastry to handle and must be chilled before using.

1 cup all-purpose flour	1 stick butter, cubed
pinch of salt	few drops of vanilla extract
¼ cup sugar	
⅓ cup (2 oz) ground almonds	1 medium egg, beaten

MAKES A 9″ PIE CRUST

Sift the flour, salt and sugar into a bowl, then mix in the ground almonds. Rub in the butter until the mixture resembles fine bread crumbs. Make a well in the center, add the vanilla and the beaten egg. Mix together with a round-bladed knife to form a dough. Turn onto a lightly floured surface and knead for a few seconds until smooth. Wrap the dough in plastic wrap and chill for 30–40 minutes until firm, before using.

Crème Pâtissiére

A rich, thick custard used as a filling for cakes, small pastries, and tarts. Its light, smooth, cool texture contrasts and complements both sponge cakes and pastries alike. The basic mixture is flavored with vanilla, but it can also be flavored with liqueurs, chocolate, coffee, orange, or lemon.

Add liqueurs, such as Grand Marnier, Kirsch or brandy to the cold custard, but don't add too much or the custard will become thin.

Chocolate, coffee, orange, or lemon rind should be heated with the milk before it is added to the egg mixture.

It is always best to make the custard the day before it is to be used, to ensure that it is thoroughly chilled; for a firmer setting, a little gelatin can be added – where required, this is indicated in the recipes.

3 egg yolks	1 teaspoon vanilla extract
⅓ cup sugar	1 egg white
3 tablespoons all-purpose flour, sifted	⅔ cup heavy cream
1¼ cups milk	MAKES ABOUT 2 CUPS

Beat the egg yolks and 1½ tablespoons sugar in a bowl until pale and thick. Fold in the flour.

Put the milk and the vanilla into a saucepan and bring almost to a boil. Gently whisk the hot milk into the egg and flour mixture. Strain the mixture, through a nylon sieve, back into the pan.

Cook the custard over a gentle heat, stirring, until the mixture thickens. Pour the hot custard into a clean bowl, then cover the surface closely with plastic wrap to prevent a skin forming. Allow the custard to cool completely, but not to set too firmly.

Beat the egg white until stiff, then gradually beat in the remaining sugar. Whip the cream until thick.

Whisk the cooled custard until smooth, then gradually fold in the egg white then the cream. Cover the crème pâtissière with plastic wrap and chill before using.

Crème Chantilly

The addition of sugar and vanilla extract before whipping, turns heavy cream into crème Chantilly, making the cream smoother and more flavorful. It is used extensively for filling and decorating cakes, large and small pastries, and desserts.

1¼ cups very fresh heavy cream, well chilled	½-1 teaspoon vanilla extract
1 tablespoon confectioners' sugar, sifted	MAKES ABOUT 2 cups

Put the cream into a well-chilled bowl with the sugar and vanilla extract to taste, then whip until the cream forms soft peaks, or a little thicker if required for piping. Take care not to overwhip the cream or it will turn buttery and be unusable.

Apricot Glaze

Apricot glaze is used for glazing pastries and tarts to make them look more attractive; the addition of a little Kirsch or Grand Marnier gives extra flavor.
If using homemade jam add a little water; most commercial jams are already quite thin and will melt down very easily but do use a good quality preserve rather than ordinary jam for the best taste. Raspberry and strawberry preserves can be used in exactly the same way to make a red glaze.

1 cup apricot preserve	1–2 tablespoon Kirsch, optional

Put the preserves into a small saucepan and heat gently, stirring all the time, until melted. Sieve the preserves through a nylon sieve into another small clean saucepan. Add the Kirsch, then bring to a boil, stirring. The glaze should always be at boiling point when used to ensure that it sets well.

Apricot glaze will keep well, stored in an airtight jar in a cool place, ready to be heated when required for glazing.

Index